W9-BHG-495

A VISUAL EXPLORATION OF SCIENCE

A VISUAL GUIDE TO EVOLUTION AND GENETICS

Rosen
YA
New York

SOL90 EDITORIAL STAFF

This edition published in 2019 by:
The Rosen Publishing Group, Inc.
29 East 21st Street
New York, NY 10010

Cataloging-in-Publication Data

Names: Editorial Sol90 (Firm).
Title: A visual guide to evolution and genetics / edited by the Sol90 Editorial Staff.
Description: New York : Rosen YA, 2019. | Series: A visual exploration of science | Includes glossary and index.
Identifiers: ISBN 9781508186274 (pbk.) | ISBN 9781508186281 (library bound)
Subjects: LCSH: Evolution (Biology)—Juvenile literature. | Evolution—Juvenile literature. | Genetics—Juvenile literature.
Classification: LCC QH367.1 V578 2019 | DDC 576.8—dc23

Manufactured in the United States of America

Project Management: Nuria Cicero
Editorial Coordination: Alberto Hernández, Joan Soriano, Diana Malizia
Proofreaders: Marta Kordon, Edgardo D'Elio
Layout: Laura Ocampo

Photo Credits: Age Fotostock, Getty Images, Science Photo Library, Graphic News, ESA, NASA, National Geographic, Latinstock, Album, ACI, Cordon Press, Shutterstock.com

Illustrators: Guido Arroyo, Pablo Aschei, Carlos Francisco Bulzomi, Gustavo J. Caironi, Hernán Cañellas, Leonardo César, José Luis Corsetti, Vanina Farías, Manrique Fernández Buente, Joana Garrido, Celina Hilbert, Inkspot, Jorge Ivanovich, Iván Longuini, Isidro López, Diego Martín, Jorge Martínez, Marco Menco, Marcelo Morán, Ala de Mosca, Diego Mourelos, Laura Mourelos, Pablo Palastro, Eduardo Pérez, Javier Pérez, Ariel Piroyansky, Fernando Ramallo, Ariel Roldán, Marcel Socías, Néstor Taylor, Trebol Animation, Juan Venegas, Constanza Vicco, Coralia Vignau, Gustavo Yamin, 3DN, 3DOM studio.

Contents

Yesterday, Today, and Tomorrow

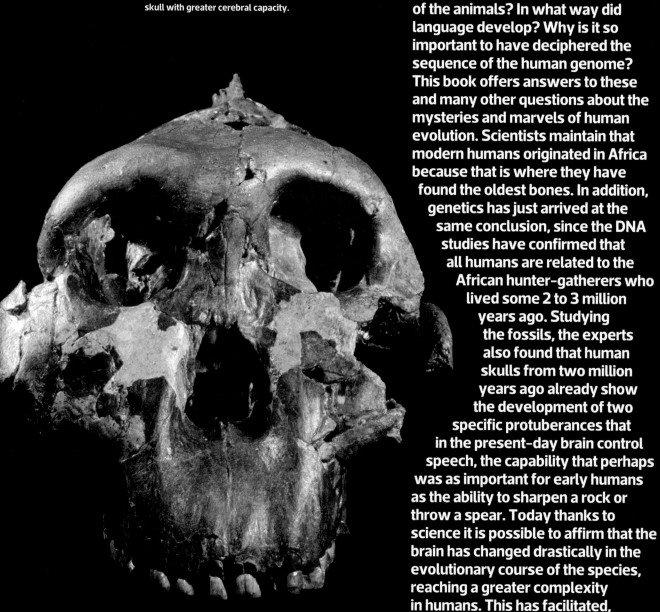

FACES OF THE PAST
The skull of Australopithecus (below) shows a reduced cerebral portion and a strong jaw. To the right, Cro-Magnon, a representative of modern humans, exhibits a more evolved skull with greater cerebral capacity.

When did humans appear? What is it that makes us different from the rest of the animals? In what way did language develop? Why is it so important to have deciphered the sequence of the human genome? This book offers answers to these and many other questions about the mysteries and marvels of human evolution. Scientists maintain that modern humans originated in Africa because that is where they have found the oldest bones. In addition, genetics has just arrived at the same conclusion, since the DNA studies have confirmed that all humans are related to the African hunter-gatherers who lived some 2 to 3 million years ago. Studying the fossils, the experts also found that human skulls from two million years ago already show the development of two specific protuberances that in the present-day brain control speech, the capability that perhaps was as important for early humans as the ability to sharpen a rock or throw a spear. Today thanks to science it is possible to affirm that the brain has changed drastically in the evolutionary course of the species, reaching a greater complexity in humans. This has facilitated, among other things, the capacity to store information and the flexibility in behavior that makes a human an incredibly complex individual. The purpose of this book is to tell you and show you in marvelous images many of the answers that people have found throughout history, through their successes, failures, and new questions. These new questions have served to shape the world in which we live, a world whose scientific, technological, artistic, and industrial development surprises and at times frightens us. History is full of leaps. For thousands of years nothing may happen, until all of a sudden some new turn or discovery gives an impulse to humankind. For example, with the domestication of animals and the cultivation of plants, a profound societal revolution occurred. This period of prehistory, called the Neolithic, which dates to 10,000–11,000 years ago, opened the way for the development of civilization. With the possibility of obtaining food without moving from place to place, the first villages were established and produced great demographic growth.

The book that you have in your hands explains all this in an accessible way. Here you will also find information about the latest discoveries related to the structure of DNA, the molecule of heredity, that opens new areas of investigation. It contributes to the study of clinical and forensic medicine and posits new questions about the origin of life and where we are headed as humans. The possibility of untangling the sequence of the human genome is not only important in trying to explain why we are here and to explore our evolutionary past, but it also offers the possibility of altering our future. In the decades to come, the application

of genetic therapy will allow, among other things, the cure of genetic disorders caused by defective genes. In addition, the alternative of knowing beforehand what diseases a person could develop will be extremely valuable in the field of health, because we will be able to choose examinations and treatments according to individual needs. Another very promising area of medical research involves the use of stem cells that have the unique capacity to be used at some future date to regenerate organs or damaged tissues. Do not wait any longer. Turn the page and begin to enjoy this book, which may be a point of departure in your own adventure in learning. ●

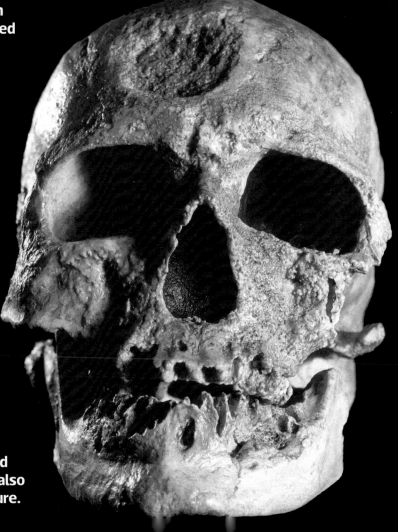

Myths and Scientific Evidence

The evolution of species cannot be considered an isolated event in itself but rather the result of a complex and constant interaction among different elements. It represents not simply an unlimited number of genetic mutations but also changes in the environment, fluctuations in sea level, varying contributions of nutrients, and possibly

BLACK SHEEP
The black color of this specimen is a clear expression of genes, the function of which is to determine different traits.

factors such as the reversal of the Earth's magnetic field or the impact of large meteorites on the Earth's surface. In this chapter, we tell you stories and legends from some of the most remote places in the world as well as various scientific theories concerning the origin of life and of human beings. Some of the curious facts and photos in these pages will surprise you. ●

Various Beliefs

Before the emergence of scientific theories, most people in the world had their own versions of the origin of the world and of humankind expressed primarily in the form of myths. Many of them have reached us through the teachings of different religions. In many cases, the origin of the world and of humankind relates to one or several creator gods or demigods; in other cases, there is no beginning and no end. With regard to the origin of the human race (the word "human" shares the same root as the Latin word *humus*, meaning "earth"), there is a Central African legend that links humans to monkeys. ●

PROPOR
The size o
heads rev
the impor
given to t
symbols.

The Matter of Creation

▶ India is a multicultural, agricultural society where much of its thousand-year-old rituals still exist. However, its sacred texts were written at very different times, from 1,000 BC (the Rigveda) to the 16th century AD (the Puranas), and they offer different versions of the origin of humankind. One of them even tells of a primal man (Purusha) from whom gods originated and from whose body parts the different castes arose. In this culture, social classes are strongly differentiated.

YORUBA MASK
represents the
two sexes.

BRAHMA,
THE CREATOR
Another version states that the first human emerged directly from the god Brahma, whose human image is represented by this statue.

HERMAPHRODITE
According to more recent texts (from the 15th century), the first person Brahma created was called Manu, and he was a hermaphrodite. The story goes that as a result of his dual sexual condition, he had a number of children, both males and females.

How Monkeys Became Human

▶ In Africa, the continent that is today believed to be the cradle of the human species, there are several myths that account for the origin of mankind. One of these actually interweaves it with the origin of the monkey. It tells how the creator god Muluku made two holes in the Earth from where the first woman and the first man sprouted and how he taught them the art of agriculture, but they neglected it and the Earth dried up. As punishment, Muluku banished them to the rainforest and gave them monkey tails, and he removed the tails from monkeys and ordered them to be "human."

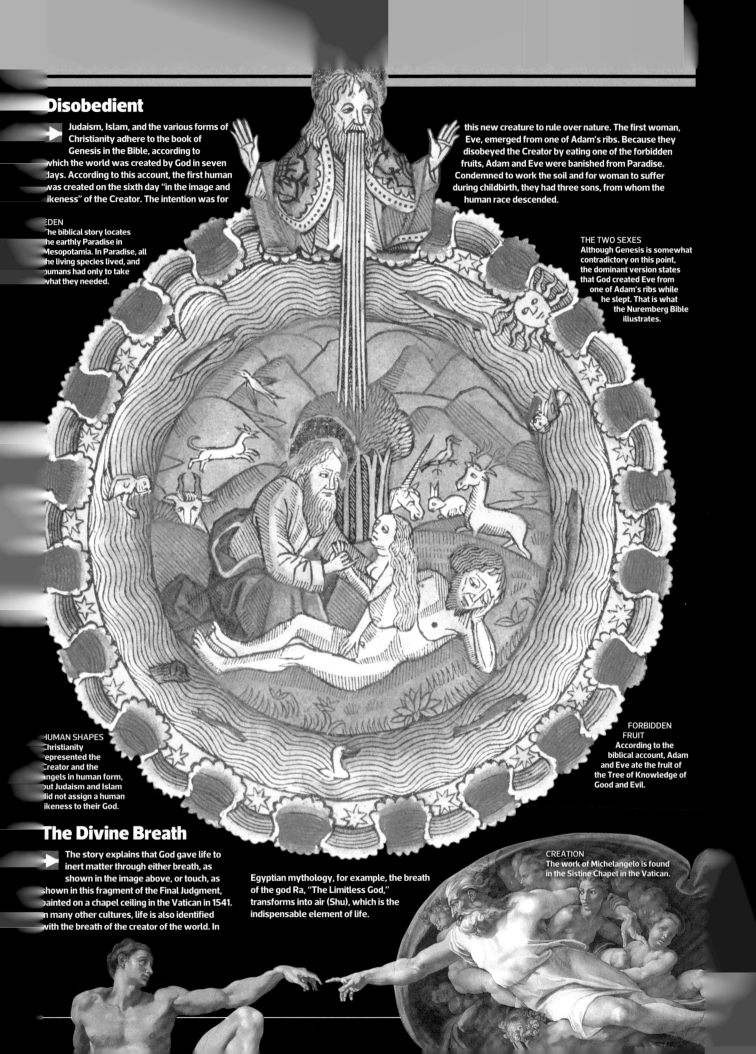

Disobedient

Judaism, Islam, and the various forms of Christianity adhere to the book of Genesis in the Bible, according to which the world was created by God in seven days. According to this account, the first human was created on the sixth day "in the image and likeness" of the Creator. The intention was for this new creature to rule over nature. The first woman, Eve, emerged from one of Adam's ribs. Because they disobeyed the Creator by eating one of the forbidden fruits, Adam and Eve were banished from Paradise. Condemned to work the soil and for woman to suffer during childbirth, they had three sons, from whom the human race descended.

EDEN
The biblical story locates the earthly Paradise in Mesopotamia. In Paradise, all the living species lived, and humans had only to take what they needed.

THE TWO SEXES
Although Genesis is somewhat contradictory on this point, the dominant version states that God created Eve from one of Adam's ribs while he slept. That is what the Nuremberg Bible illustrates.

HUMAN SHAPES
Christianity represented the Creator and the angels in human form, but Judaism and Islam did not assign a human likeness to their God.

FORBIDDEN FRUIT
According to the biblical account, Adam and Eve ate the fruit of the Tree of Knowledge of Good and Evil.

The Divine Breath

The story explains that God gave life to inert matter through either breath, as shown in the image above, or touch, as shown in this fragment of the Final Judgment, painted on a chapel ceiling in the Vatican in 1541. In many other cultures, life is also identified with the breath of the creator of the world. In Egyptian mythology, for example, the breath of the god Ra, "The Limitless God," transforms into air (Shu), which is the indispensable element of life.

CREATION
The work of Michelangelo is found in the Sistine Chapel in the Vatican.

Evolution Is a Matter of Time

Toward the 18th century, scientific progress demanded a different explanation of the myth of the origin of the world and of life. Even before Darwin, the work of naturalists and the discovery of fossils pointed to the fact that time, measured not in years but in millennia, runs its course, allowing each species to become what it is. Genetic mutations occur through the generations, and interaction with the environment determines that the most suitable traits will be transmitted (natural selection) and that a population will evolve in relationship to its ancestors. The idea is not related to "improvement" but rather to change as the origin of diversity, to the ramifications of evolutionary lines tracked through paleontological or genetic studies. ●

A Common History

Animals that look very different may be built according to the same basic body design. For example, dogs, whales, and human beings are mammals. All have the same skeletal design with a spinal column and two pairs of limbs connected to it. This suggests that they all share a common ancestor. In mammals, the bones of the limbs are the same even if they are morphologically different from one another.

KEY

● Humerus ● Ulna ● Radius ● Carpal ● Metacarpal

In mammals, the basic design of the limb is very similar—an upper bone (humerus), followed by a pair of lower ones (radius and ulna), and then the carpals and metacarpals with up to five digits.

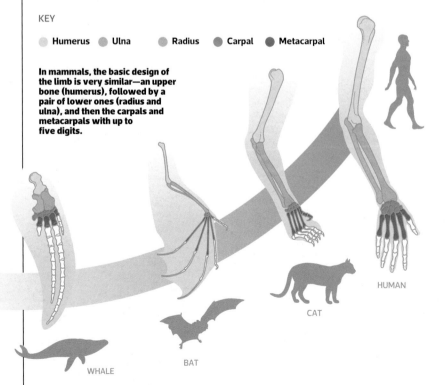

WHALE

BAT

CAT

HUMAN

A

Fossil Remains

The evidence of past life is registered in fossils, preserved between layers of sedimentary rocks deposited one on top of another through geological eras. An analysis of fossils helps determine their age. Through studies of fossil populations, it is possible to learn about the structure of old communities, the reason given species became extinct, and how animals and plants evolved over time.

PETRIFIED FOSSILS
This head of an *Albertosaurus* discovered as a fossil can be studied using geological or biomolecular analyses.

Only one fossil is found for every

20,000
extinct
species.

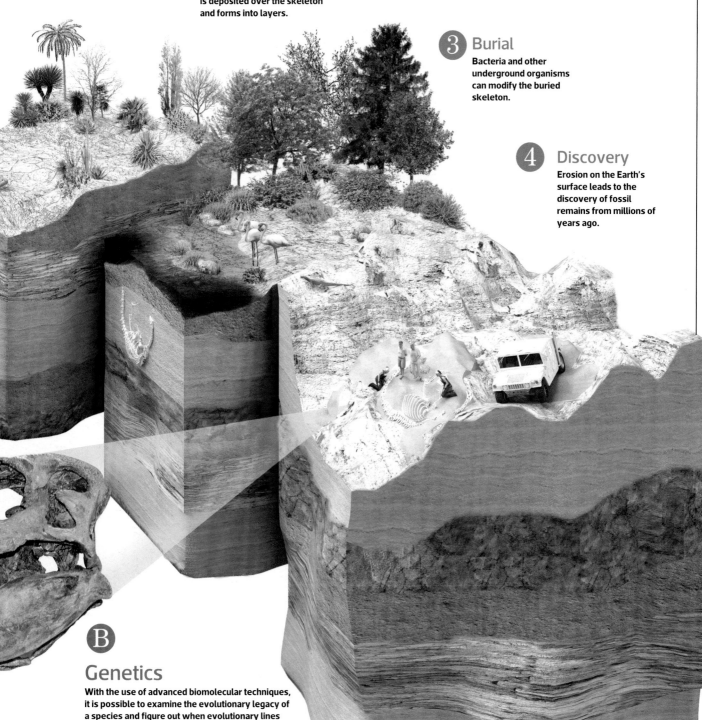

1 Dinosaurs
Animals that lived millions of years ago left behind their fossil remains.

2 Sediment
Sediment from rivers and seas is deposited over the skeleton and forms into layers.

150 million years
is the typical age of dinosaur fossils.

3 Burial
Bacteria and other underground organisms can modify the buried skeleton.

4 Discovery
Erosion on the Earth's surface leads to the discovery of fossil remains from millions of years ago.

B Genetics
With the use of advanced biomolecular techniques, it is possible to examine the evolutionary legacy of a species and figure out when evolutionary lines diverged. Many anthropologists use mitochondrial DNA (which is inherited from the mother) to reconstruct human evolution. This type of analysis is also used to reconstruct the family trees of animals.

Evolutionary Processes

n addition to natural selection, the famous theory developed by Charles Darwin in the 19th century, there are other evolutionary processes at work at the microevolutionary scale, such as mutations, genetic flow (i.e., migration), and genetic drift. However, for evolutionary processes to take place, there must be genetic variation— modifications to the proportion of certain genes (alleles) within a given population over time. These genetic differences can be passed on to subsequent generations, thereby perpetuating the evolutionary process.

A

Natural Selection

This is one of the basic mechanisms of evolution. It is the process of species survival and adaptation to changes in the environment, and it involves shedding some traits and strengthening others. This revolutionary transformation takes place when individuals with certain traits have a survival or reproduction rate higher than that of other individuals within the same population, thus passing along these genetic traits to their descendants.

GENETIC VARIATION IN THE GIRAFFE

1

COMPETITION
In the 19th century, because of the theories of Darwin and Lamarck, among others, it was believed that the ancestors of giraffes had short necks.

2

MUTATION
On the basis of spontaneous mutations, some individuals developed longer necks, allowing them to survive in the competition for food.

3

ADAPTATION
Their long necks allowed them to survive and pass along this trait to their descendants.

THE GEOMETER MOTH AND ITS ENVIRONMENT
The genes of geometer moths, which live on tree bark lichen, have different versions (alleles) for gray and black. At the start of the Industrial Revolution in England, the gray moth was better able to camouflage itself than the black moth and thus better able to avoid predators. All this changed with the emergence of pollution, which blackened tree trunks.

1

MIMESIS
The population of moths with gray alleles grows larger because of its camouflage.

DREPANA FALCATARIA was found hidden on a tree in Norfolk (U.K.) in 1994.

B

Mutation

This involves the modification of the sequences of genetic material found in DNA. When a cell divides, it produces a copy of its DNA; however, this copy is sometimes imperfect. This change can occur spontaneously, such as from an error in DNA replication (meiosis) or through exposure to radiation or chemical substances.

THE PROCESS
A mutation is a discrepancy in the DNA copy.

COPY WITH MUTATION

CORRECT COPY

C

Genetic Flow

The transfer of genes from one population to another occurs particularly when two populations share alleles (different versions of genes). For example, when a population of brown beetles mixes with a population of green beetles, there might be a higher frequency of brown beetle genes in the green beetles. This also occurs when new alleles combine as a result of mixing.

3
SURVIVAL
The population of moths with black alleles grows and surpasses the population with gray alleles.

D

Genetic Drift

This is a gradual change in the genetic makeup of a population that is not linked to the environment. Unlike natural selection, this is a random process that does not generate adaptations. Genetic drift is present in small populations in which each individual carries within itself a large portion of the genetic pool, especially when a new colony is established (the founding effect), or when a high number of individuals die and the population rebuilds from a smaller genetic pool than before (the bottleneck effect).

2
POLLUTION
Moths with black alleles find themselves better adapted to their new environment, which is the result of industrial pollution.

95%

THE PROPORTION OF BLACK MOTHS FOUND IN URBAN AREAS

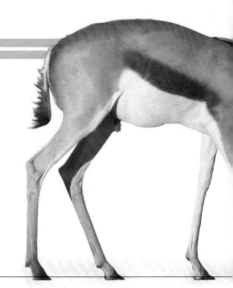

To Live or Die

Coevolution is a concept used by scientists to describe the evolutionary process from a group perspective, because no single species has done it in isolation. On the contrary, different levels and types of relationships were established through time between species, exerting changing pressures on their respective evolutionary paths. Natural selection and adaptation, both processes that every species has undergone to the present, depend on these relationships. ●

Types of Relationships

If the evolution of each species were an isolated event, neither the relationships nor the adaptations that together generate coevolution would exist. In fact, in the struggle for survival, some species react to the evolutionary changes of other species. In the case of a predator, if its prey were to become faster, the hunt would become more difficult and a demographic imbalance would develop in favor of the prey. Therefore, the speed of each depends on the mutual pressure predator and prey exert on each other. In nature, different types of relationships exist that are not always clear or easily discernible given the complexity they can acquire through the process of coevolution. These range from noninteraction to predation, from cooperation to competition and even parasitism.

A ## Commensalism

is a relationship between two species of organisms in which one benefits and the other is neither harmed nor helped. There are several types of commensalism: phoresy, when one species attaches itself to another for transportation; inquilinism, when one species is housed inside another; and metabiosis, such as when the hermit crab lives inside the shell of a dead snail.

B ## Mutualism

is a type of interspecific relationship in which both species derive benefit. It might seem as if this is an agreement between parties, but it is actually the result of a long and complicated process of evolution and adaptation. There are numerous examples of mutualism, although the most famous is the cattle egrets of Africa (*Bubulcus ibis*), which feed on the parasites of large herbivores such as the buffalo and the gnu. To the extent that the egrets obtain their food, the herbivores are rid of parasites.

The Environment

INTERACTS WITH COEVOLUTION, SUCH AS WHEN AN ENVIRONMENTAL CHANGE FAVORS OR HARMS A GIVEN SPECIES.

C ## Parasitism

is defined as an asymmetric relationship in which only one of the organisms (the parasite) derives benefit. It is an extreme case of predation that entails such fundamental adaptations where the parasite, which enters by various means, might even live inside its host. Such is the case of the African buffalo, which can have a worm called *Elaeophora poeli* lodged in its aorta.

COMPETITION
There is also competition within a species, whether for food or for mating partners.

D Competition

takes place when two or more organisms obtain their resources from a limited source. This is a relationship that has one of the strongest impacts on natural selection and the evolutionary process. There are two types of competition. One occurs through interference, which is when an action limits another species' access to a resource—for example, when the roots of a plant prevent another plant from reaching nutrients. The other type of competition is through exploitation, typical among predators such as lions and cheetahs that prey on the same species. In this second type, the principle of competitive exclusion is also at play, since each species tends to eliminate its competition.

Debate

FOR EVOLUTIONARY SCIENTISTS, IT IS NOT CLEAR WHETHER THE DRIVING FORCE OF EVOLUTION IS COOPERATION OR COMPETITION. THE LATTER NOTION HAS BEEN FAVORED BY THE SCIENTIFIC COMMUNITY SINCE THE 19TH CENTURY.

E

Predation

is the interspecies relationship in which one species hunts and feeds on another. It is important to understand that each party exerts pressure on and regulates the other. There are specific instances of predation in which the hunter impacts only one type of prey or those in which it feeds on different species. The degree of adaptation depends on this distinction. The lion, the zebra, and the kudu form an example of the latter case.

The Critical Point

One of the big issues posed by the theory of evolution is how a new species arises. This presumes that a population becomes separated from other individuals within its group (when, for example, it lives under conditions different from those of its parents) and ceases to interact with them. Through the generations, the isolated individuals will experience genetic mutations that give rise to phenotypic changes completely different from those experienced by the original population to which they once belonged, and they develop traits so distinct that they become a new species. From an evolutionary perspective, this is how one can understand the constant emergence of new lineages and the growing diversity of living beings. ●

The origin of new species

▶ Individuals of the same species look alike and breed among themselves, but not with those of other species. In speciation, two or more species arise from a single species (cladogenesis), or several fertile individuals arise from the crossbreeding of two different species (hybridization), although the latter is much less frequent in nature. Cladogenesis can arise out of geographical isolation or simply through a lack of genetic flow between groups of individuals of the same species, even if they are present in the same territory.

THE HONEYCREEPERS

New species can arise from a common ancestor. All the Hawaiian honeycreepers evolved from the same ancestor. They have different colors and bills. The original species is now extinct. The diet of the honeycreeper changed with each new generation.

Akiapola'au
Hemignathus munroi
searches for insects under-neath the barks of trees.

Apanane
Himatione sanguinea
feeds on insects and ohia flower nectar.

Iiwi
Vestiaria coccinea
feeds exclusively on nectar.

Bills

Their varying shapes explain the adaptation of each bird to the changes in its diet.

Maui Parrotbill
Pseudonestor xanthophrys
removes bark in search of beetles.

Hawaii Amakihi
Hemignathus virens
has a curved bill and feeds on nectar.

Nihoa Finch
Telespiza ultima
can shatter seeds with its hard beak.

Selection

In spite of their differences, dogs are so similar to each other that they can breed with each other. They are in the same species. But selective breeding is a good example of how differentiation is favored, except that in nature it takes a longer time to do this. Selection can be disruptive, when two populations separate and become differentiated; directional, when the dominant traits of a population change; or stabilizing, when variations diminish and individuals become more similar to each other.

Gray Wolf
Canis lupus
The ancestor of the dog is very intelligent and social. It travels in packs of 8 to 12 members.

Siberian Husky
Canis familiaris

Unlike the German shepherd, which evolved through 10,000 years of human breeding, the Siberian husky preserves traits closer to those of the gray wolf, which are the ancestors all dogs.

German Shepherd
Canis familiaris
This strong, trainable dog herds cattle and sheep tirelessly and with great intelligence.

Origin of Life

An effort of imagination is needed to see just how new complex life-forms are on Earth. For millions of years the development of life was completely static. Suddenly one day this stagnant world exploded unexpectedly with new forms of life, an effect called the Cambrian explosion. The fossil record shows an impressive

proliferation of incredibly varied life-forms. The emergence of new species in the oceans took place at the same time as the massive extinction of stromatolites, which had dominated the Proterozoic Eon up to that point. In this chapter you will also discover how new creatures continued to appear that over time populated the face of the Earth. ●

Through Time

Geologic structures and fossils have been used by scientists to reconstruct the history of life on our planet. Scientists believe that the Earth was formed about 4.6 billion years ago and that the first living beings, single-celled organisms, appeared about one billion years later. From that time, the Earth has registered the emergence, evolution, and extinction of numerous species. Thanks to the study of fossils paleontologists can provide an account of plants and animals that have disappeared from the Earth. ●

HOW IT STARTED

FORMATION OF THE CRUST. The oldest known rocks date to about four billion years ago and the oldest known crystals to about 4.6 billion years ago.

LAVA BECAME ROCK. The first terrestrial surface was a thin layer with scattered volcanoes that spouted very light lava that came from the Earth's interior. As the lava cooled, it hardened and thickened the early crust.

PRESENCE OF OXYGEN. Life on Earth was dependent on the presence of oxygen, which established itself in the atmosphere and over the surface some 2.1 billion years ago. Oxygen makes possible the formation of fundamental compounds, such as water and carbon dioxide, whose molecular model is shown here.

THE FIRST EVIDENCE. Stromatolites, fossils that date back some 3.5 billion years, are one of the first evidences of life on the planet. These formations correspond to single-celled algae that lived underwater. In this image you can see a fossil of *Collenia*, found in the United States.

A CURIOUS FOSSIL. This fossil of mawsonite found in the Ediacara of Australia is one of the oldest fossils from a metazoan, or multicellular, animal. It is at least 600 million years old. Cnidarians are well-represented among Ediacaran fossils.

ANAEROBIC AND AQUATIC LIFE. The first atmosphere had no oxygen; the first organisms (bacteria) used anaerobic respiration.

PROTECTED LIFE. The most common animal life-forms of the Cambrian Period already showed well-defined body structures. Many were protected by valves or shells.

THE CAMBRIAN EXPLOSION. Numerous multicellular species suddenly appeared.

SCALES. The image shows the scales of a Lepidotus, a type of archaic fish. These were covered by a hard and shiny substance similar to enamel. Today most reptiles and fish have scales.

CONQUEST OF EARTH. The first land species appeared during the Silurian Period. Plants invaded the first sedimentary areas, and crustaceans came out of the water.

METALDETES had a calcareous structure similar to that of sponges. They lived in the Cambrian sea.

CRINOID FOSSIL. The fossils from these archaic marine invertebrates were typical of the Silurian Period and are widely distributed in sedimentary rocks.

MASSIVE EXTINCTIONS. Great climatic changes and other circumstances produced the first massive extinctions of species, evidenced by great banks of fossils.

THE PRESENCE OF OXYGEN. The first fish, called agnates, had no jaws. This pteraspis, found in shallow waters, belongs to the Silurian Period.

ON FOUR LEGS. This very ancient amphibian, called Acanthostega, lived during the Devonian Period.

4.6 BILLION YEARS AGO. The basic materials that formed the Earth condensed.

1 BILLION YEARS AGO. Several large continental pieces come together, forming the supercontinent Rodinia.

270 MILLION YEARS AGO. The mass of solid land is again concentrated in a single continent, called Pangea, that would become the origin of the continents we know today. Repeated glaciations took place, and the central Tethys Sea was formed.

200 MILLION YEARS AGO. Laurasia (North America, Europe, and Asia) and Gondwana (South America, Africa, India, Australia, and Antarctica) separate from each other.

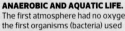

MASS EXTINCTIONS		60% OF SPECIES		80% OF SPECIES		95% OF SPECIES	
4.6-2.5 BILLION YEARS AGO	2.5 BILLION-542 MILLION YEARS AGO	542 - 488	488 - 444	444 - 416	416 - 359	359 - 299	299 - 251
ARCHEAN EON	PROTEROZOIC EON	CAMBRIAN	ORDOVICIAN	SILURIAN	DEVONIAN	CARBONIFEROUS	PERMIAN
PRECAMBRIAN TIME		**PALEOZOIC ERA**					

THE TIMELINE

Most of the history of life on the planet has had simple, single-celled organisms, such as bacteria, as the lead actors. Bacteria have survived for more than three billion years. In comparison, the reign of dinosaurs during the Mesozoic Era (about 250 to 65 million years ago) is a recent event. And the presence of humans on Earth is insignificant on this time scale.

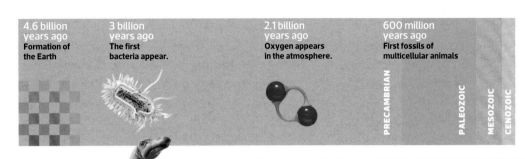

4.6 billion years ago
Formation of the Earth

3 billion years ago
The first bacteria appear.

2.1 billion years ago
Oxygen appears in the atmosphere.

600 million years ago
First fossils of multicellular animals

PRECAMBRIAN · PALEOZOIC · MESOZOIC · CENOZOIC

THE ERA OF REPTILES.
Large and small, they conquered terrestrial environments, but there were also aquatic species (such as the Icthyosaurus) and others in the air (such as the Pterosaurus).

NEW TYPES OF ANIMALS. The first mammals and birds appear on Earth. There was a great diversification of mollusks in the oceans, where species such as the nautilus survive to this day.

A CHANGING WORLD. The end of the Mesozoic Era witnessed a great climatic change with a major fall in average temperatures. This led to an era of glaciations.

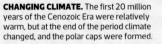

PREDATOR.
Giganotosaurus carolinii was one of the largest carnivorous dinosaurs, with a length of 50 feet (15 m). Below, a Tyrannosaurus tooth, 3 inches (8 cm).

HEAVYWEIGHT.
The heaviest of all known dinosaurs was the Barosaurus. It is calculated that it could have weighed up to 100 tons.

VERTEBRA.
This is a fossil vertebra of a *Barosaurus*. The neck was flexible thanks to the light weight of these bones.

180 MILLION YEARS AGO.
Gondwana separates, forming Africa, Antarctica, Australia, India, and South America.

CHANGING CLIMATE. The first 20 million years of the Cenozoic Era were relatively warm, but at the end of the period climate changed, and the polar caps were formed.

PRAIRIES, THE IDEAL STAGE. The spread of hominin species throughout the planet coincided with the expansion of prairies as the dominant form of vegetation.

FINALLY ALONE.
Without the threat of the large dinosaurs, birds and mammals could develop.

FEATHERED.
Titanis was a carnivorous bird. Because of its size (8.2 feet [2.5 m] tall) and its small wings, it was flightless.

SABER TEETH. Thylacosmilus resembled the felines of today, but it was a marsupial. The females had a pouch for the young, like that of kangaroos. Their teeth never stopped growing. Their fossils were found in Argentina; they lived during the Miocene and Pliocene epochs, subdivisions of the Neogene Period.

RELATIVES. The first fossils of Homo neanderthalensis were found in 1856. They had a common ancestor with Homo sapiens.

Australopithecus afarensis. A reconstruction of the head of this hominin is shown here. It was an ancestor of the human genus and lived from 3.7 million to 2.9 million years ago. With a height of 40 inches (1 m), it was smaller than modern humans. According to theory, Homo habilis descended from it.

50 MILLION YEARS AGO.
The continental masses were in positions similar to those of today. Some of the highest mountain ranges of today, the Alps and the Andes, were being formed. Simultaneously, the subcontinent of India was colliding with Eurasia to form the highest mountain range, the Himalayas.

75% OF SPECIES

251 - 200	200 - 146	146 - 65.5	65.5 - 23	SINCE 23 MILLION YEARS AGO
TRIASSIC	JURASSIC	CRETACEOUS	PALEOGENE	NEOGENE
MESOZOIC ERA			**CENOZOIC ERA**	

Chemical Processes

A lthough it is assumed today that all life-forms are connected to the presence of oxygen, life began on Earth more than three billion years ago in the form of microorganisms. They determined, and still determine today, the biological processes on Earth. Science seeks to explain the origin of life as a series of chemical reactions that occurred by chance over millions of years and that gave rise to the various organisms of today. Another possibility is that life on Earth originated in the form of microbes that reached the Earth from space, lodged, for instance, within a meteorite that fell to the Earth's surface. ●

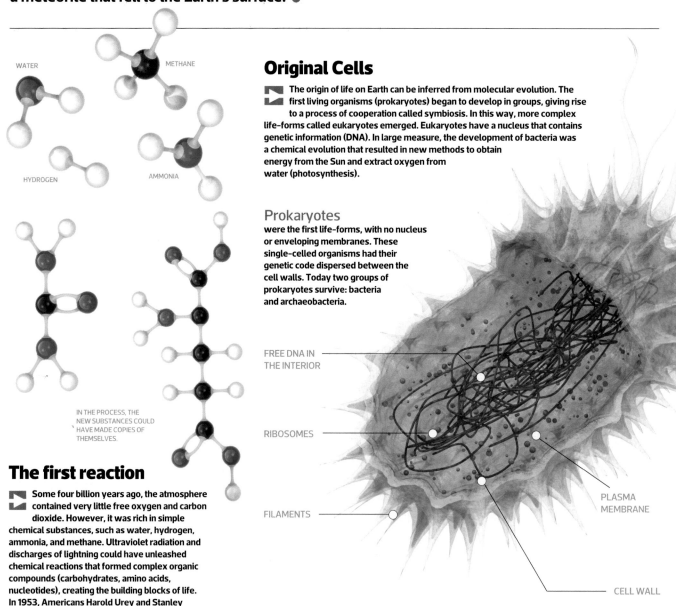

WATER

METHANE

HYDROGEN

AMMONIA

IN THE PROCESS, THE
NEW SUBSTANCES COULD
HAVE MADE COPIES OF
THEMSELVES.

Original Cells

The origin of life on Earth can be inferred from molecular evolution. The first living organisms (prokaryotes) began to develop in groups, giving rise to a process of cooperation called symbiosis. In this way, more complex life-forms called eukaryotes emerged. Eukaryotes have a nucleus that contains genetic information (DNA). In large measure, the development of bacteria was a chemical evolution that resulted in new methods to obtain energy from the Sun and extract oxygen from water (photosynthesis).

Prokaryotes

were the first life-forms, with no nucleus or enveloping membranes. These single-celled organisms had their genetic code dispersed between the cell walls. Today two groups of prokaryotes survive: bacteria and archaeobacteria.

FREE DNA IN
THE INTERIOR

RIBOSOMES

FILAMENTS

PLASMA
MEMBRANE

CELL WALL

The first reaction

Some four billion years ago, the atmosphere contained very little free oxygen and carbon dioxide. However, it was rich in simple chemical substances, such as water, hydrogen, ammonia, and methane. Ultraviolet radiation and discharges of lightning could have unleashed chemical reactions that formed complex organic compounds (carbohydrates, amino acids, nucleotides), creating the building blocks of life. In 1953, Americans Harold Urey and Stanley Miller tested this theory in the laboratory.

ARCHEAN
4.6 BILLION YEARS AGO

4.2 BILLION
YEARS AGO

4 BILLION
YEARS AGO

The Earth's atmosphere sets it aside from the other planets.

Volcanic eruptions and igneous rock dominate the Earth's landscape.

The Earth's surface cools and accumulates liquid water.

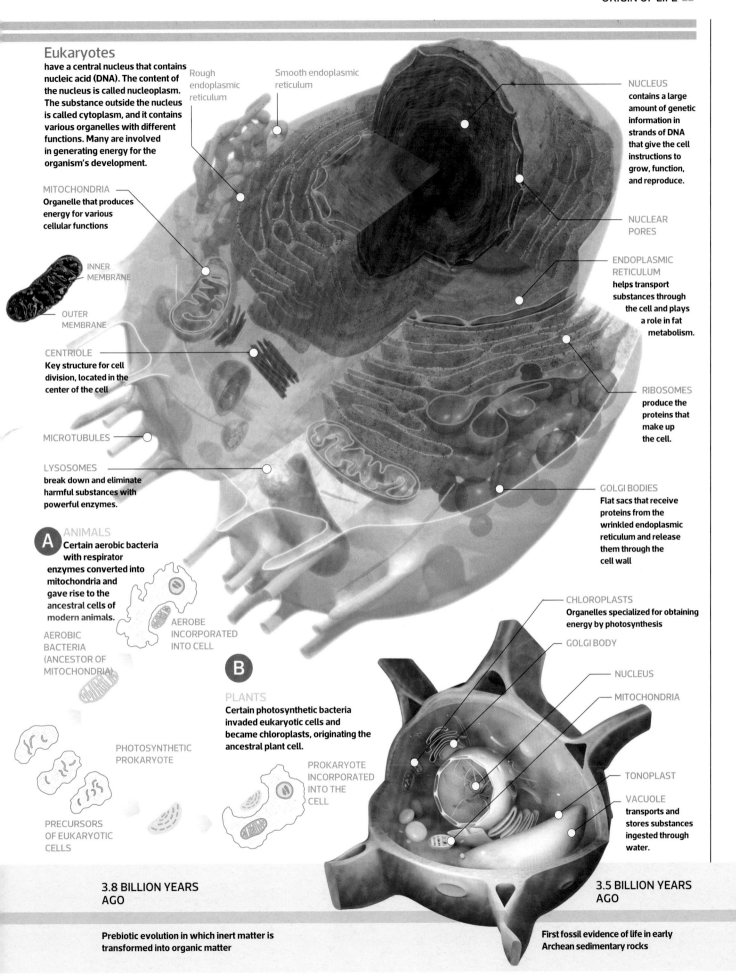

Eukaryotes

have a central nucleus that contains nucleic acid (DNA). The content of the nucleus is called nucleoplasm. The substance outside the nucleus is called cytoplasm, and it contains various organelles with different functions. Many are involved in generating energy for the organism's development.

Rough endoplasmic reticulum

Smooth endoplasmic reticulum

NUCLEUS
contains a large amount of genetic information in strands of DNA that give the cell instructions to grow, function, and reproduce.

NUCLEAR PORES

ENDOPLASMIC RETICULUM
helps transport substances through the cell and plays a role in fat metabolism.

MITOCHONDRIA
Organelle that produces energy for various cellular functions

INNER MEMBRANE

OUTER MEMBRANE

CENTRIOLE
Key structure for cell division, located in the center of the cell

MICROTUBULES

LYSOSOMES
break down and eliminate harmful substances with powerful enzymes.

RIBOSOMES
produce the proteins that make up the cell.

GOLGI BODIES
Flat sacs that receive proteins from the wrinkled endoplasmic reticulum and release them through the cell wall

A ANIMALS
Certain aerobic bacteria with respirator enzymes converted into mitochondria and gave rise to the ancestral cells of modern animals.

AEROBIC BACTERIA (ANCESTOR OF MITOCHONDRIA)

AEROBE INCORPORATED INTO CELL

B PLANTS
Certain photosynthetic bacteria invaded eukaryotic cells and became chloroplasts, originating the ancestral plant cell.

PHOTOSYNTHETIC PROKARYOTE

PROKARYOTE INCORPORATED INTO THE CELL

PRECURSORS OF EUKARYOTIC CELLS

CHLOROPLASTS
Organelles specialized for obtaining energy by photosynthesis

GOLGI BODY

NUCLEUS

MITOCHONDRIA

TONOPLAST

VACUOLE
transports and stores substances ingested through water.

3.8 BILLION YEARS AGO

3.5 BILLION YEARS AGO

Prebiotic evolution in which inert matter is transformed into organic matter

First fossil evidence of life in early Archean sedimentary rocks

Fossil Relics

The term proterozoic comes from the Greek *proteros* ("first") and *zoic* ("life") and is the name given to an interval of geologic time of about two billion years at the end of what is known as Precambrian time. The oldest fossils of complex organisms yet found, in the Ediacara fossil bed (Australia), date from the end of the Proterozoic, in the Neoproterozoic Era. It is the first evidence of multicellular organisms with differentiated tissues. It is believed that the specimens of Ediacara life were not animals but prokaryotes that were formed of various cells and did have internal cavities. Toward the end of the Proterozoic, there was a global disturbance in the carbon cycle that caused the disappearance of most complex organisms and opened the way for the great explosion of life in the Cambrian Period. ●

CHARNIA
is one of the largest fossils of the Ediacaran Period. Its flat, leaf-shaped body was supported by a disklike structure.

Primitive Species

It has been established that the animals of the Ediacara were the first invertebrates on the Earth. They appeared approximately 650 million years ago and were made up of various cells. Some had a soft flat body while others were in the form of a disk or a long strip. A relevant fact about the life of this period is that they no longer had only one cell that was in charge of feeding, breathing, and reproducing; instead, the diverse cells specialized in distinct functions.

40 inches
(100 cm)
MAXIMUM LENGTH

STROMATOLITES

are the most ancient evidence of life known on Earth, and even today they have maintained their evolutionary line. They are laminated organic-sedimentary structures, principally cyanobacteria and calcium carbonate, stuck to the substrate product of metabolic activity. They grew in mass, which led to the formation of reefs.

CALCIUM CARBONATE

CYANOBACTERIA

3 BILLION YEARS AGO

Accumulation of iron oxide on the seafloor

2.3 BILLION YEARS AGO

Extensive glaciation takes place.

3.5-4 inches
(9-10 cm)
IN DIAMETER

MAWSONITE
This species of cnidarian shifted slowly through the waters, aided by the currents. It contracted its long, thin umbrella, extending its tentacles and shooting its microscopic harpoons to capture its prey. For this, it also used a kind of poison.

CYCLOMEDUSA
Ancient circular fossil with a bump in the middle and up to five concentric ridges. Some radial segments extend along the length of the outer disks.

KIMBERELLA
An advanced metazoan from the Ediacara fauna, it is the first known organism with a body cavity. It is believed to have been similar to a mollusk. First it is found in Ediacara, Australia, and later in Russia.

8 inches
(20 cm)
IN LENGTH

1 inch
(2.5 cm)
IN LENGTH

DICKINSONIA
Usually considered an annelid worm because of its similar appearance to an extinct genus (*Spinther*). It also may be a version of the soft body of the banana coral fungus.

TRIBRACHIDIUM
It is believed that this species, developed in the form of a disk with three symmetric parts, is a distant relative to corals and to anemones.

40 inches
(100 cm)
IN LENGTH

2 inches
(5 cm)
IN DIAMETER

600 MILLION YEARS AGO

Multicellular marine organisms called Ediacara fauna develop.

The Cambrian Explosion

Unlike the previous development of microbial life, the great explosion of life that emerged in the Cambrian some 500 million years ago gave rise to the evolution of a diversity of multicellular organisms (including mollusks, trilobites, brachiopods, echinoderms, sponges, corals, chordata) protected by exoskeletons or shells. It is believed that this group of organisms represents the characteristic fauna of the Cambrian. The Burgess Shale fossil bed in British Columbia (Canada) holds a large number of fossils of soft-bodied animals of the period and is one of the most important fossil formations in the world.

Burgess Shale

Located in Yoho National Park in the Canadian province of British Columbia, Burgess Shale is a celebrated fossil bed found in 1909 by the American paleontologist Charles Walcott. Burgess Shale offers a unique look at the explosion of Cambrian life. It contains thousands of very well-preserved fossilized invertebrates, including arthropods, worms, and primitive chordata, some with their soft parts intact.

0.4 inch
(10 mm)

Provided with a strong exoskeleton, the *Anomalocaris* was a true terror in the Cambrian seas.

SPONGES
They grew primarily on the seabed in Burgess Shale and frequently developed alongside algae of diverse species, sizes, and shapes.

PRIAPULIDS
Benthic worms that live buried in sand and in the mud of shallow water as well as in deep water. There are about 15 species.

0.8 inch
(2 cm) **IN LENGTH**

CAMBRIAN
(542 TO 488 MILLION YEARS AGO)

CAMBRIAN BEGINS

The increased presence of oxygen permitted the formation of shells.

ANOMALOCARIS

The largest plundering arthropod known of that time, it had a circular mouth, appendages that allowed it to strongly grasp its prey, and fins along the length of both sides that were used for swimming. In comparison to other organisms, it was a true giant of Burgess Shale.

Comparison to human scale

24 inches
(60 cm)
THE LENGTH REACHED BY THIS SPECIES

PIKAIA

One of the first chordates, similar to an eel, with a tail in the shape of a flipper. It is the oldest known ancestor to vertebrates.

4 inches
(10 cm) long
INCLUDING THE TAIL

MARELLA

Small swimming arthropod that was probably an easy prey for predators in Burgess Shale.

4 inches
(10 cm) in length
TO THE EXTREMITIES

HALLUCIGENIA

Had a defense system based on long spines that simultaneously served as feet for its movement.

1.2 inches
(3 cm) maximum length
OF THIS ARTHROPOD

THE EVOLUTIONARY EXPLOSION

The Cambrian originated a great variety of body designs.

CORAL REEFS

Coral reefs are formed by the calcareous skeletons of innumerable soft bodied animals.

Conquest of the Earth

T he Paleozoic Era (ancient life) was characterized by successive collisions of continental masses, and the occupation of their interior lakes made possible the appearance of primitive terrestrial plants, the first fish adapted to freshwater, and amphibians, highlighting a key evolutionary event: the conquest of the terrestrial surface some 360 million years ago. For this process, diverse mechanisms of adaptation were necessary, from new designs of vascular plants and changes in the bone and muscular structures to new systems of reproduction. The appearance of reptiles and their novel amniotic egg meant the definitive colonization of the land by the vertebrates, just as the pollen made plants completely independent of water. ●

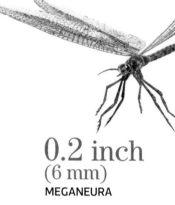

0.2 inch
(6 mm)
MEGANEURA

New breed of fish

▶ After the decline of the trilobites and the appearance of corals, crinoids, bryozoa, and pelecypods came the fish with external bony shields and no jaws, which are the first—known vertebrates. During the Silurian Period, the cephalopods and jawed fish abounded in a globally warm climate. The adaptation of the fish as much to freshwater as saltwater coincided with the predominance of boned fish, from which amphibians developed.

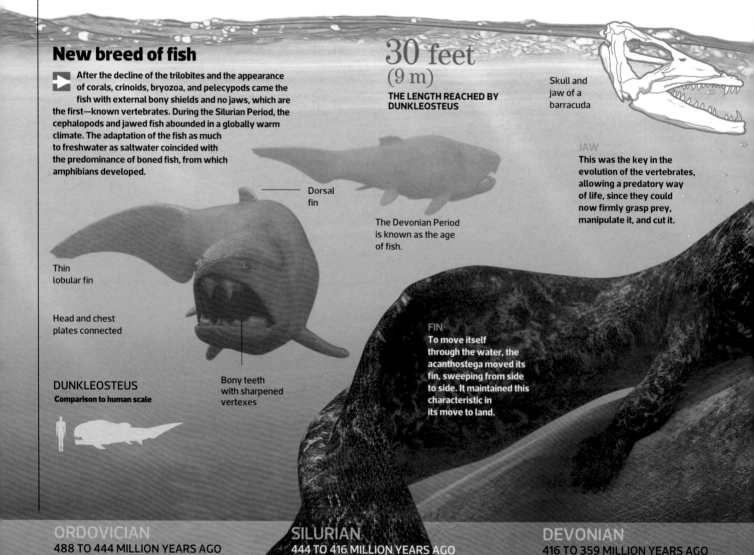

30 feet
(9 m)
THE LENGTH REACHED BY DUNKLEOSTEUS

Skull and jaw of a barracuda

Dorsal fin

The Devonian Period is known as the age of fish.

JAW

This was the key in the evolution of the vertebrates, allowing a predatory way of life, since they could now firmly grasp prey, manipulate it, and cut it.

Thin lobular fin

Head and chest plates connected

FIN

To move itself through the water, the acanthostega moved its fin, sweeping from side to side. It maintained this characteristic in its move to land.

DUNKLEOSTEUS
Comparison to human scale

Bony teeth with sharpened vertexes

ORDOVICIAN
488 TO 444 MILLION YEARS AGO

SILURIAN
444 TO 416 MILLION YEARS AGO

DEVONIAN
416 TO 359 MILLION YEARS AGO

The first land organisms appear—lichens and bryophytes.

Great coral reefs and some types of small plants

Vascular plants and arthropods form diverse terrestrial ecosystems.

From fins to limbs

The amphibian evolution facilitated the exploration of new sources of foods, such as insects and plants, and an adaptation of the respiratory system for the use of oxygen in the air. For this purpose, the aquatic vertebrates had to modify their skeleton (a greater pelvic and pectoral waist) and develop musculature. At the same time, the fins transformed into legs to permit movement on land.

35-47 inches
(90-120 cm)
MAXIMUM LENGTH

FIRST FISH AND PLANTS

The success of the vertebrates in the colonization of land came in part from the evolution of the amniotic egg covered in a leathery membrane. In the evolution of plants, pollen made them independent of water.

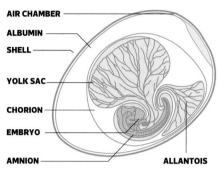

AIR CHAMBER
ALBUMIN
SHELL
YOLK SAC
CHORION
EMBRYO
AMNION
ALLANTOIS

0.2 inch
(6 mm)

ACANTHOSTEGA

Comparison to human scale

DORSAL SPINE
Its system of joints, called zygapophyses, between the vertebrae helps to maintain the rigidity of the dorsal spine.

PREDATOR
The development of a large mouth allowed it to hunt other vertebrates.

DEVELOPMENT OF VESSELS IN PLANTS

The need to transport water from the root to the stem and to transport photosynthetic products in the opposite direction in plants induced the development of a system of internal vessels. Reproduction based on pollen achieved the definite conquest of the terrestrial environment.

Pollen guarantees reproduction.

Internal vessel conductors

BONE STRUCTURE
Only three bones (humerus, cubitus, and radius) formed the bone support of the legs. Unlike fish, it had a type of mobile wrist and eight fingers that moved all at once like a paddle.

CARBONIFEROUS
359 TO 299 MILLION YEARS AGO

Land tetrapods and winged insects appear.

PERMIAN
299 TO 251 MILLION YEARS AGO

Large variety of insects and vertebrates on land

The Reign of the Dinosaurs

F rom abundant fossil evidence, scientists have determined that dinosaurs were the dominant form of terrestrial animal life during the Mesozoic Era. There was a continual change of dinosaur species. Some of them lived during the three periods of the Mesozoic Era, others throughout two, and some in only one. Unlike the rest of the reptiles, the legs of dinosaurs were placed not toward the side but under the body, as they appear in mammals. This arrangement, together with its bone structure (a femur articulated to a hollow pelvis) significantly aided its locomotion. In their evolution, the dinosaurs also developed such defensive features as horns, claws, hornlike beaks, and armor. It was long believed that dinosaurs were cold-blooded; nevertheless, the dominant hypothesis today is that they were warm-blooded. They mysteriously became extinct toward the end of the Cretaceous Period. ●

The *Plateosaurus* walked on four legs but could reach elevated foliage with support from its tail.

Up to 33 feet
(10 m) PLATEOSAURUS (FLAT REPTILE)

COMPARATIVE SIZE

Triassic Period

Following the massive extinction and biological crisis at the end of the Permian Period, only a relatively few species of plants and animals were able to survive. In the Triassic, the regeneration of life slowly began. Mollusks dominated in marine environments, and reptiles dominated on land. As for plants, families of ferns, conifers, and bennettitales appeared during the middle and late Triassic.

MAMMALS

At the end of the Triassic, there are traces of mammals, which evolved from cynodont reptiles. Among the mammalian characteristics that made their appearance were elongated and differentiated teeth and a secondary palate.

FERN   PALM   CONIFER   GINGKO

TRIASSIC
251 TO 200 MILLION YEARS AGO

The equatorial supercontinent of Pangea forms.

Jurassic Period

The increase in sea levels inundated interior continental regions, generating warmer and more humid environments that favored the development of life. The reptiles adapted to diverse environments, and the dinosaurs developed greatly. During this period, there are examples of herbivore dinosaurs existing together with carnivorous dinosaurs. Freshwater environments were favorable for the evolution of invertebrates, amphibians, and reptiles such as turtles and crocodiles. The first birds emerged.

BIPEDALISM
The *Allosaurus*, a giant therapod carnivore, was one of the first species to move about on two legs.

HORSETAIL   CONIFER

Up to 30 feet (9 m) STEGOSAURUS (ROOFED LIZARD)

Cretaceous Period

In this period, carnivorous dinosaurs appeared with claws curved in the shape of a sickle, specially designed to gut its prey. A prime example is the claw of *Baryonyx*. It measures 12 inches (30 cm), a disproportionate length for an animal 30 feet (9 m) in length. During the Cretaceous Period, the evolution of insects and birds continued, and flora that made use of pollination developed. Nevertheless, this period was marked both by a revolution in the seas (the appearance of new groups of predators, such as teleost fish and sharks) and by a revolution on land (the extinction of the dinosaurs about 65 million years ago).

Up to 50 feet (15 m)
GIGANOTOSAURUS (GREAT SOUTHERN LIZARD)

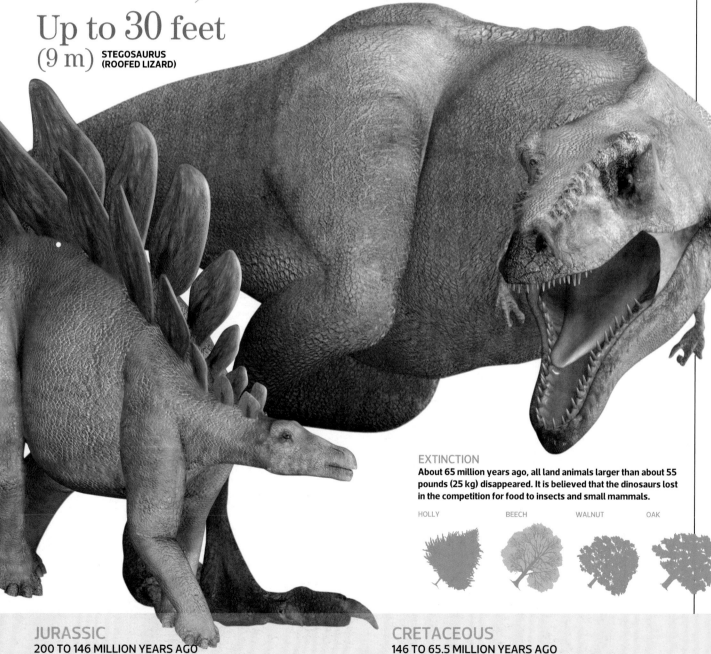

EXTINCTION
About 65 million years ago, all land animals larger than about 55 pounds (25 kg) disappeared. It is believed that the dinosaurs lost in the competition for food to insects and small mammals.

HOLLY   BEECH   WALNUT   OAK

JURASSIC
200 TO 146 MILLION YEARS AGO

Fragmentation of Pangea and
increase in sea level

CRETACEOUS
146 TO 65.5 MILLION YEARS AGO

Present-day oceans and
continental masses are defined.

The End of the Dinosaurs

Dinosaurs reigned over the Earth until about 65 million years ago. All of a sudden they died out because of a drastic change in the conditions that made their life possible. The most reasonable hypothesis for this change attributes it to the collision of a large asteroid or comet with the Earth. The resulting fire devastated all of what today are the North and South American continents. The impact raised huge dust clouds that remained suspended in the air for months, darkening the planet. At the same time, sulfur, chlorine, and nitrogen was mixed into dense clouds, causing killing acid rains. ●

More Theories About the "K-T Boundary"

▶ The period between the Cretaceous and Paleogene periods, known as the "K-T boundary," marks the end of the era of the dinosaurs. Although the impact theory is widely accepted, other theories suggest that there was a great change in climate that caused dinosaurs to become extinct very slowly as the shallow seas withdrew from solid land. According to the defenders of these theories, the dinosaurs were being reduced in variety and number throughout a period that lasted millions of years. The large meteorite of Chicxulub, according to this hypothesis, would have fallen some 300 thousand years before the end of the Cretaceous Period. It has also been hypothesized that mammals proliferated before the extinction and fed on reptile eggs, or that the plants eaten by the large sauropods succumbed to diseases.

6 miles
(10 km)
WAS THE DIAMETER OF
THE METEORITE THAT
FELL IN CHICXULUB.

K-T BOUNDARY
65 MILLION YEARS AGO

Sudden climatologic change,
65 million years ago

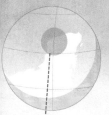

Chicxulub, Mexico

 VOLCANIC ERUPTIONS
Another theory relates the massive extinction with the appearance of prolonged volcanic eruptions on Earth that emitted asphyxiating gases and darkened the skies with dust. Thousands of cubic miles of volcanic rock found on a plateau in Deccan, India, support this theory.

C **SPACE CATACLYSM**
Every 67 million years, the Solar System crosses through the plane of the Milky Way. At those times some stars in the Milky Way can cause comets to escape from the Oort cloud and enter the inner Solar System. It is possible that one of these bodies could have impacted the Earth.

A Profound Evidence

In the Mexican town of Chicxulub, on the Yucatán Peninsula, there is a depression 62 miles (100 km) in diameter that is attributed to the impact of a meteorite about 65 million years ago. The layers of rock that make up the soil support this theory and make it possible to see what occurred before and after the impact.

50%
OF LIVING SPECIES
became extinct at
the same time.

POST-EXTINCTION
sediments
accumulated in the
Cenozoic Era.

DUST AND ASH
from the impact of
the fireball

EJECTED ROCK
material from the
crater that has
settled

PRE-EXTINCTION
sediments with
fossils of dinosaurs

IN THE ROCKS
In the region of the
Yucatán, rocks made
of meteorite fragments
are commonly found
compressed among
the (darker) mineral
sediments.

50 million
ATOMIC BOMBS
is the equivalent, according
to calculations, of the energy
unleashed by the impact in
Chicxulub.

PALEOGENE
65.5 TO 23 MILLION YEARS AGO

Beginning of the Cenozoic Era
which extends to the present.

Land of Mammals

A fter the extinction of the large dinosaurs at the end of the Mesozoic Era, mammals found the opportunity to evolve until becoming sovereigns of the Earth. The Cenozoic Era, which began 65.5 million years ago, also saw the appearance and evolution of plants with flowers, and large mountain chains of today (the Himalayas, the Alps, and the Andes) formed. Within the zoological class of mammals, primates appeared, as did the *Homo* genus, the immediate ancestors of humans, toward the end of the era. ●

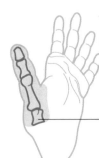

CONTINENTS OF
THE PAST

PRESENT-DAY
CONTINENTS

The Class that Defines an Era

Some 220 million years ago, the mammaliaformes appeared, which today are all extinct. More similar to reptiles, they already had larger skulls and were beginning to raise their stomachs from the ground with the strength of their limbs. And 100 million years ago, the two predominant surviving suborders appeared—the marsupials (which remain only in Oceania, with the exception of the American opossum) and the placentals (which colonized the entire Cenozoic world).

200
million
years

MAMMALS HAVE
BEEN ON LAND

Ancestors of Humans

Primates are mammals that are characterized by binocular vision, the large relative size of their brains, and the prehensile limbs that allowed them, among others things, to take to the branches of trees and make use of objects as rudimentary tools. The first primates (called *Purgatorius*) appeared in North America in the Paleocene Epoch. The oldest fossils of monkeys (anthropoids) date from some 53 million years ago, but the origin is still uncertain.

MORGANUCODON

Extinct insectivorous rodent of the Jurassic (200 million years ago)

COMPARATIVE SIZE

Its total length was 6 inches (15 cm), and it weighed from 1 to 2 ounces (30–50 g).

SHORT TAIL
The appendage of the vertebral column, it ended in a point. This differentiates it from present-day rodents.

Theropithecus oswaldi

COMPARATIVE
SIZE

PRIMATES
APPEAR IN THE
CENOZOIC ERA.

Size similar to a human, 3 to 6 feet (1–2 m)

PREHENSILE THUMB
One finger opposite the rest, predecessor to the thumb of humans, allowed this European monkey of the Pliocene to manipulate objects (5 million years ago).

LONG CLAWS
With these it hunted insects and dug holes to hide from dinosaurs.

PALEOGENE
65.5 TO 23 MILLION YEARS AGO

Mammals are represented by marsupials, prosimians, and ungulates.

NEOGENE
FROM 23 MILLION YEARS AGO

Hominoids disperse from Africa to all over the world.

TAIL
They used it for climbing equilibrium. In American monkeys, the tail was prehensile: it allowed them to hang from branches.

New Plants
At the beginning of the Cenozoic Era flowering plants diversified and became prevalent in Earth's forests except in cold regions.

SYCAMORE
(PALEOCENE)

FICUS
(EOCENE)

GRASSES
(PLIOCENE)

60
million
years ago

SINCE THE APPEARANCE OF PRIMATES ON EARTH

SPRUCE
(PLEISTOCENE)
Establishment of the conifers

LONG FINGERS
are what first permitted the anthropoids to hold onto the branches and move through the trees.

RANUNCULUS
(PLEISTOCENE)
One of the first plants with flowers

PLEISTOCENE
FROM 1.8 MILLION TO 12,000 YEARS AGO

Development of the first
Homo sapiens.

HOLOCENE
FROM 12,000 YEARS AGO TO THE PRESENT

First fossil records of
Homo sapiens sapiens

The Tree of Life

Here is a visual representation to explain how all living beings are related. Unlike genealogical trees, in which information supplied by families is used, phylogenetic trees use information from fossils as well as that generated through the structural and molecular studies of organisms. The construction of phylogenetic trees takes into account the theory of evolution, which indicates that organisms are descendants of a common ancestor. ●

Eukaryota

This group consists of species that have a true nucleus in their cellular structure. It includes unicellular and multicellular organisms, which are formed by specialized cells that do not survive independently.

Animals

Multicellular and heterotrophic. Two of their principal characteristics are their mobility and their internal organ systems. Animals reproduce sexually, and their metabolism is aerobic.

Archaea

These organisms are unicellular and microscopic. The majority are anaerobic and live in extreme environments. About one half of them give off methane in their metabolic process. There are more than 200 known species.

Plants

Multicellular autotrophic organisms; they have cells with a nucleus and thick cellular walls that are grouped in specialized tissues. They carry out photosynthesis by means of chloroplasts.

CNIDARIANS
include species such as the jellyfish and corals.

BILATERAL
Symmetrical bilateral organisms.

EURYARCHAEOTA
Halobacteria salinarum

KORARCHAEOTA
The most primitive of the archaea.

NOT VASCULAR
No internal vessel system.

VASCULAR
Internal vessel system.

VERTEBRATES
have a vertebral column, a skull that protects the brain, and a skeleton.

MOLLUSKS
include the octopus, snails, and oysters.

CRENARCHAEOTA
live in environments with high temperatures.

WITH SEED
Some have exposed seed and some have flower and fruit.

SEEDLESS
They are small plants with simple tissues.

TETRAPODS
Animals with four limbs.

CARTILAGINOUS FISH
include the rays and sharks.

Relationships

The scientific evidence supports the theory that life on Earth has evolved and that all species share common ancestors. However, there are no conclusive facts about the origin of life. It is known that the first life-forms must have been prokaryotes, or unicellular beings, whose genetic information is found anywhere inside their cell walls. From this point of view, the archaea are prokaryotes, as are bacteria. For this reason, they were once considered to be in the same kingdom of living things, but certain characteristics of genetic transmission places them closer to the eukaryotes.

ANGIOSPERM
With flower and fruit. More than 250,000 species form this group.

AMPHIBIANS
When young they are water dwellers; later they live on land.

GYMNOSPERM
With naked seeds; cycadophytes were examples.

Amniotes

The evolution of this feature allowed the tetrapods to conquer land and to adapt to its distinct environments. In amniote species the embryo is protected in a sealed structure called the amniotic egg. Among mammals, only monotremes continue to be oviparous; however, in the placental subclass, to which humans belong, the placenta is a modified egg. Its membranes have transformed, but the embryo is still surrounded by an amnion filled with amniotic fluid.

Bacteria

Unicellular organisms that live on surfaces in colonies. Generally they have one cellular wall composed of peptidoglycans, and many bacteria have cilia. It is believed that they existed as long as three billion years ago.

COCCALS
The pneumococcals are an example.

BACILLUS
Escherichia coli has this form.

SPIRILLUM
In the form of a helicoid or spiral

VIBRIO
Found in saltwater

Protista

A paraphyletic group, it includes the species that cannot be classified in any other group. There are, therefore, many differences among protista species, such as algae and the amoeba.

10,000,000
SPECIES OF ANIMALS ARE CALCULATED TO INHABIT THE EARTH IN THEIR DISTINCT ENVIRONMENTS.

Fungi

Cellular heterotrophic organisms with cell walls thickened with chitin. They carry out digestion externally and secrete enzymes to reabsorb the resulting molecules.

BASIDIOMYCETES
include the typical capped mushrooms.

ZYGOMYCETES
reproduce through zygospores.

ABOUT
5,000
SPECIES OF MAMMALS ARE INCLUDED IN THREE GROUPS.

ASCOMYCETES
Most species are grouped here.

CHYTRIDIOMYCETES
can have mobile cells.

DEUTEROMYCETES
Asexual reproduction.

ARTHROPODS
have an external skeleton (exoskeleton). Their limbs are jointed appendages.

INSECTS
The greatest evolutionary success.

MYRIAPODS
Millipedes and centipedes.

Cladistics

This classification technique is based on the evolutionary relationship of species coming from similar derived characteristics and supposes a common ancestor for all living species. The results are used to form a diagram in which these characteristics are shown as branching points that have evolved; at the same time, the diagram places the species into clades, or groups. Although the diagram is based on evolution, its expression is in present–day characteristics and the possible order in which they developed. Cladistics is an important analytical system, and it is the basis for present–day biological study. It arises from a complex variety of facts: DNA sequences, morphology, and biochemical knowledge. The cladogram, commonly called the tree of life, was introduced in the 1950s by the German entomologist Willi Hennig.

BONY FISH
have spines and a jaw.

CRUSTACEANS
Crabs and ocean lobsters.

ARACHNIDS
Spiders, scorpions, and acarids.

AMNIOTES
Species that are born from an embryo inside an amniotic egg.

MAMMALS
The offspring are fed with mother's milk.

PLACENTAL
The offspring are born completely developed.

Humans

Humans belong to the class Mammalia and specifically share the subclass of the placentals, or eutherians, which means that the embryo develops completely inside the mother and gets its nutrients from the placenta. After birth, it depends on the mother, who provides the maternal milk in the first phase of development. Humans form part of the order Primates, one of the 29 orders in which mammals are divided. Within this order, characteristics are shared with monkeys and apes. The closest relatives to human beings are the great apes.

BIRDS AND REPTILES
Oviparous species. Reptiles are ectothermic (cold-blooded).

MARSUPIALS
The embryo finishes its development outside of the mother.

TURTLES
The oldest reptiles.

CROCODILES
Scaly and with long bodies.

SNAKES
Also classified with lizards.

MONOTREMES
The only oviparous mammals. They are the most primitive.

Human Evolution

Homo sapiens, the name that scientifically designates our species, is the result of a long evolutionary process that began in Africa during the Pliocene Epoch. Very few fossils have been found, and there are no clear clues about what caused the amazing development of the culture. Some believe that a change in the

brain or vocal apparatus permitted the emergence of a complex language. Other theories hypothesize that a change in the architecture of the human mind allowed *Homo sapiens* to use imagination.

What is certain is that hunting and gathering was a way of life for 10,000 years until people formed settlements after the Ice Age and cities began to emerge. ●

Human Evolution

P erhaps motivated by climatic change, some five million years ago the species of primates that inhabited the African rainforest subdivided, making room for the appearance of the hominins, our first bipedal ancestors. From that time onward, the scientific community has tried to reconstruct complex phylogenetic trees to give an account of the rise of our species. DNA studies on fossil remains allow us to determine their age and their links with different species. Each new finding can put into question old theories about the origin of humans. ●

Primates That Talk

The rise of symbolic language, which is a unique ability of humans, is a mystery. But the evolution of the speech apparatus in humans has been decisive. The human larynx is located much lower than in the rest of the mammals. This characteristic makes it possible to emit a much greater variety of sounds.

THE PHYLOGENETIC TREE

This cladogram (map of emergence of new species from previous ones) shows the relationship of the *Homo* genus to the other species of primates.

MAN CHIMPANZEE GORILLA ORANGUTAN

1 MYA

5 MYA

10 MYA

15 MYA

20 MYA
(MILLION YEARS AGO)

Gorillas, chimpanzees, and hominins had a common ancestor at least five million years ago.

NOT-SO-DISTANT RELATIVES

There are various uncertainties and disagreements among paleontologists about how the evolutionary tree for hominins branches out. This version is based on one created by paleoanthropologist Ian Tattersall.

Australo-pithecus

PRECURSOR
This ape was the first true hominin but is extinct today.

UPRIGHT POSTURE
Walking on two legs led to a weakening of the neck muscles and a strengthening of the hip muscles.

FREE ARMS

BIPEDALISM
requires less energy to move and leaves the hands free.

Homo habilis

THE GREAT LEAP
Its brain was much greater, and there were substantial anatomical changes.

GROWTH
It is calculated that the growth of the brain is 44 percent larger with respect to *Australopithecus*, an enormous development in relation to the body.

ABILITY
It already was using sticks and rocks as tools.

BONES
Those of the hands and legs are very similar to those of modern human beings.

A. ramidus   A. anamensis   A. afarensis

ARDIPITHECUS   *AUSTRALOPITHECUS*

P. aethiopicus

A. africanus

???

A. garhi

4 MILLION YEARS AGO

PARANTHROPUS

TOOLS FOR SPEAKING

The larynx of humans is located much lower than in chimpanzees and thus allows humans to emit a greater variety of sounds.

CHIMPANZEE

MAN

LARYNX

VOCAL CORDS

AND FOR THINKING

The evolution of the brain has been essential for the development of language and other human capacities. Greater cranial capacity and nutrition have had physiological influences.

CHIMPANZEE

MAN

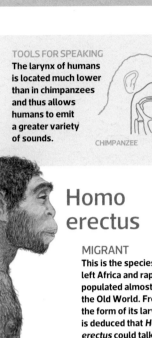

Homo erectus

MIGRANT

This is the species that left Africa and rapidly populated almost all the Old World. From the form of its larynx, it is deduced that *Homo erectus* could talk.

MUSCLES

Some prominent muscle markings and thick reinforced areas of the bones indicate that the body of *H. erectus* could support strong movement and muscle tension.

THICKNESS

Its bones, including the cranium, were thicker than those in previous species.

SIZE

It already had the stature of *Homo sapiens* but was stronger.

Homo neander-thalensis

HUNTER-GATHERER

Very similar to *H. sapiens*; nevertheless, it is not its ancestor, but a species that emerged from *H. erectus*.

CHEST

The rib cage opened slightly outward.

ADAPTATION

Its short, robust physique shows good adaptation to cold climates.

Homo sapiens

CULTURAL ANIMAL

The only surviving species of the *Homo* genus. Its evolution took place not through genetics but through culture.

STABLE MOVEMENT

With the femur forming an angle toward the inside, the center of the body mass is rearranged; this permits stable bipedal movement.

P. boisei

P. robustus

H. habilis

H. rudolfensis

H. ergaster

H. heidelbergensis

H. erectus

H. neanderthalensis

H. sapiens

2 MILLION YEARS AGO

1 MILLION YEARS AGO

TODAY

HOMO

First Humans

LOCATION OF THE REMAINS OF THE FIRST HOMINIDS

AFRICA

The *Australopithecus* were the first humanlike creatures who could walk in an upright posture with their hands free, as indicated by the fossils found in Tanzania and Ethiopia. It is believed that climatic changes, nutritional adaptations, and energy storage for movement contributed to bipedalism. In any case, their short legs and long arms are seen as indications that they were only occasional walkers. Their cranium was very different from ours, and their brain was the size of a chimpanzee's. There is no proof that they used stone tools. Perhaps they made simple tools with sticks, but they lacked the intelligence to make more sophisticated utensils. ●

Adaptation to the Environment

The climatic changes that occurred during the Miocene probably transformed the tropical rainforest into savannah. Various species of hominins left their habitats in the trees and went down to the grasslands in search of food. It is conjectured that the first hominins began to stand up to see over the grasslands.

BIPEDALISM
By walking on two feet, they were able to free their upper limbs while they moved.

ADAPTED PELVIS
Morphological changes in the pelvis, sacrum, and femur made these bones similar to those in modern humans.

KNEE
Unlike chimpanzees, the rim of the femur had an elliptical shape like that in the human knee.

AUSTRALOPITHECUS AFARENSIS

GORILLA   H. SAPIENS

SPECIAL TEETH
They had large incisors like spatulas in front, and the teeth became arranged in the form of an arch.

DORSAL SPINE
had many curves to maintain balance. Given that monkeys do not have lumbars, the weight of the body falls forward.

TOE
Whereas in chimpanzees the big toe is used to grasp, the position of the big toe and the foot arch in hominins supported movement in a bipedal posture.

GORILLA   HUMAN

Archaeological Findings

The fossil skull of a child was found in 1924 in the Taung mine (South Africa). The remains included the face with a jaw and tooth fragments as well as skull bones. The brain cavity had been replaced with fossilized minerals. Later, in 1975, footprints of hominins were found in Laetoli (Tanzania). It is believed that more than three million years ago, after a rain that followed a volcanic eruption, various specimens left their tracks in the moist volcanic ash.

SKULL OF TAUNG
Had a round head and strong jaw. Its cranial cavity could house a brain (adult) of 26 cubic inches (440 cu cm).

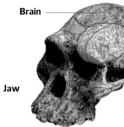

Brain

Jaw

2.5
million years ago

LAETOLI
In 1975 in Laetoli (Tanzania), tracks of hominins that archaeologists found in fossilized volcanic ash provided evidence of hominins walking on two legs (bipedalism).

3.6
million years ago

AUSTRAL OPITHECUS AFARENSIS

AUSTRALOPITHECUS ANAMENSIS

4.2 to 3.9 million years ago. Primitive hominin with wide molars.

AUSTRALOPITHECUS AFRICANUS

3 to 2.5 million years ago. Globular skull with greater cerebral capacity.

PARANTHROPUS AETHIOPICUS

Approximately 2.5 million years ago. Robust skull and solid face.

● AUSTRALOPITHECUS
ANAMENSIS

● PARANTHROPUS
AETHIOPICUS

● AUSTRALOPITHECUS
AFRICANUS

● PARANTHROPUS
ROBUSTUS

● PARANTHROPUS
BOISEI

Australopithecus afarensis

Considered the oldest hominin, it inhabited
eastern Africa between three and four million
years ago. A key aspect in human evolution
was the bipedalism achieved by *A. afarensis*.
The skeleton of "Lucy," found in 1974, was
notable for its age and completeness.

3 million years ago

COMPARATIVE SIZE

3.6 FEET
(1.1 M)

6 FEET (1.8 M)

THE SKELETON OF LUCY

This hominid found in Ethiopia had the size
of a chimpanzee, but its pelvis allowed it to
maintain an upright position.

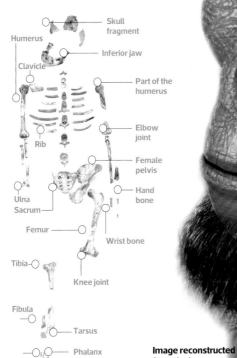

Skull
fragment

Humerus

Inferior jaw

Clavicle

Part of the
humerus

Elbow
joint

Rib

Female
pelvis

Ulna

Hand
bone

Sacrum

Femur

Wrist bone

Tibia

Knee joint

Fibula

Tarsus

Phalanx

Metatarsus

Image reconstructed
from the bones
of Lucy.

PARANTHROPUS
BOISEI

2.2 to 1.3 million years ago. Skull adapted
for consumption of tough vegetables.

PARANTHROPUS
ROBUSTUS

1.8 to 1.5 million years ago.
Very robust, bony appearance.

Use of Tools

The emergence of *Homo habilis*, which had a more humanlike appearance than *Australopithecus*, in eastern Africa showed important anatomical modifications that allowed advancement, especially in the creation of various stone tools, such as flaked pebbles for cutting and scraping and even hand axes. The bipedal posture for locomotion was established, and the first signs of language appeared. Stone technology became possible thanks to the notable increase in brain size in *Homo habilis*. In turn, the anatomic development of *Homo erectus* facilitated its migration toward areas far from its African origins, and it appears to have populated Europe and Asia, where it traveled as far as the Pacific Ocean. *Homo erectus* was capable of discovering fire, a vital element that improved human nutrition and provided protection from the cold. ●

Homo habilis

The appearance of *Homo habilis* in eastern Africa between 2 and 1.5 million years ago marked a significant advancement in the evolution of the human genus. The increased brain size and other anatomical changes together with the development of stone technology were substantive developments in this species, whose name means "handy man." Although it fed on carrion, it was still not capable of hunting on its own.

THE BRAIN
The cranial cavity of *Homo habilis* was larger than that of *Australopithecus*, reaching a cerebral development of between 40 and 50 cubic inches (650–800 cu cm). It is believed that this characteristic was key in developing the capacity of making tools, considering that it had half the brain size of modern humans.

1
CARVING
The first step was to select rocks and scrape them until sharp.

2
REMOVING
A "stone hammer" was used to sharpen the edges of the tools.

THIS CARVED ROCK IS THE OLDEST KNOWN TOOL.

2 MILLION YEARS AGO	1.7 MILLION YEARS AGO	1.5 MILLION YEARS AGO
Appearance of *Homo habilis* in eastern Africa.	*Homo erectus* is the first hominin to leave its habitat.	*Homo habilis* disappears because of unknown causes.

ASIA

AFRICA

MAP OF LOCATIONS
AND MIGRATIONS

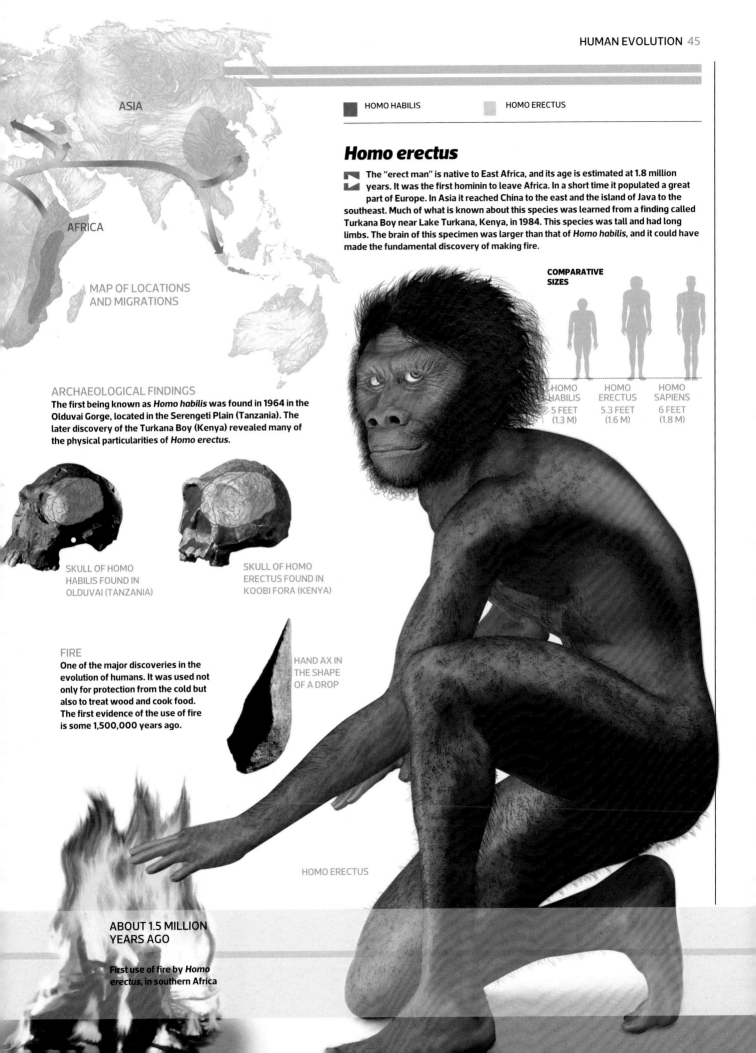

■ HOMO HABILIS   ▨ HOMO ERECTUS

Homo erectus

The "erect man" is native to East Africa, and its age is estimated at 1.8 million years. It was the first hominin to leave Africa. In a short time it populated a great part of Europe. In Asia it reached China to the east and the island of Java to the southeast. Much of what is known about this species was learned from a finding called Turkana Boy near Lake Turkana, Kenya, in 1984. This species was tall and had long limbs. The brain of this specimen was larger than that of *Homo habilis*, and it could have made the fundamental discovery of making fire.

COMPARATIVE
SIZES

HOMO
HABILIS
5 FEET
(1.3 M)

HOMO
ERECTUS
5.3 FEET
(1.6 M)

HOMO
SAPIENS
6 FEET
(1.8 M)

ARCHAEOLOGICAL FINDINGS

The first being known as *Homo habilis* was found in 1964 in the Olduvai Gorge, located in the Serengeti Plain (Tanzania). The later discovery of the Turkana Boy (Kenya) revealed many of the physical particularities of *Homo erectus*.

SKULL OF HOMO
HABILIS FOUND IN
OLDUVAI (TANZANIA)

SKULL OF HOMO
ERECTUS FOUND IN
KOOBI FORA (KENYA)

FIRE

One of the major discoveries in the evolution of humans. It was used not only for protection from the cold but also to treat wood and cook food. The first evidence of the use of fire is some 1,500,000 years ago.

HAND AX IN
THE SHAPE
OF A DROP

HOMO ERECTUS

**ABOUT 1.5 MILLION
YEARS AGO**

First use of fire by *Homo erectus*, in southern Africa

Able Hunters

D escendants of *Homo heidelbergensis*, the Neanderthals were the first inhabitants of Europe, western Asia, and northern Africa. Diverse genetic studies have tried to determine whether it is a subspecies of *Homo sapiens* or a separate species. According to fossil evidence, Neanderthals were the first humans to adapt to the extreme climate of the glacial era, to carry out funerals, and to care for sick individuals. With a brain capacity as large or larger than that of present-day humans, Neanderthals were able to develop tools in the style of the Mousterian culture. The cause of their extinction is still under debate. ●

ASIA

AFRICA

INDIAN OCEAN

MAP OF SITES

Homo neanderthalensis

The Middle Paleolithic (400,000 to 30,000 years ago) is dominated by the development of *Homo neanderthalensis*. In the context of the Mousterian culture, researchers have found traces of the first use of caves and other shelters for refuge from the cold. Hunters by nature, *H. neanderthalensis* created tools and diverse utensils, such as wooden hunting weapons with sharpened stone points.

They lived in

shelters made of mammoth bones and covered with skins.

60,000 years ago

THE AGE OF SOME NEANDERTHAL DISCOVERIES

Graves

Much is known about the Neanderthals because they buried their dead.

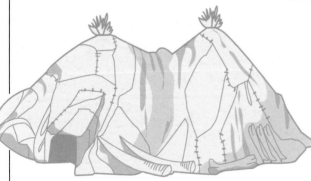

MAN—HUNTER

Males were dedicated to the search for food, while the women looked after children. It is believed that Neanderthals hunted large prey over short distances. They used wooden spears with stone points and probably jumped on the prey.

100,000 years ago
TOOLS FOUND

Rocks for cutting and scraping

Tools for tanning hides

600,000 YEARS AGO

Homo heildebergensis is in Europe, part of Asia, and Africa.

400,000 YEARS AGO

Wooden spears found in Germany and the United Kingdom date back to this time.

160,000 YEARS AGO

Homo neanderthalensis lives in the Ice Age in Europe and western Asia.

HOMO
NEANDERTHALENSIS

HOMO
HEIDELBERGENSIS

Humans of the Ice Age

Characterized as the caveman of the Ice Age, *Homo neanderthalensis* was able to use fire and diverse tools that allowed it to work wood, skins, and stones, among other materials. They used the skins to cover themselves from cold and to build shelter, and the stones and the wood were key materials in the weapons used for hunting. The bone structure of their fossils reveals a skull with prominent ciliary arcs, sunken eyes, a wide nose, and large upper teeth, probably used to grasp skins and other objects during the process of rudimentary manufacture.

PHYSICAL CONTEXT
The bones in the hand made it possible to grasp objects much more strongly than modern man can.

COMPARATIVE SIZE

5.4 FEET
(1.65 M)

6 FEET
(1.8 M)

GREATER CRANIAL CAPACITY
In comparison to modern humans, Neanderthals had a larger brain capacity.

Prominent
superciliary
arch

Wide nose
**To endure the
hardships of
the climate**

Skull found in La
Chapelle-aux-Saints
(France)

98 cubic inches
(1,600 cu cm) cranial capacity

150,000 YEARS AGO

25,000 YEARS AGO

**First *Homo sapiens*
found in Africa**

***Homo neanderthalensis* becomes
extinct from unknown causes.**

Direct Ancestors

The origin of the human species is still in debate, even though scientists have been able to establish that *H. sapiens* is not directly related to the Neanderthals. The most accepted scientific studies for dating Neanderthal fossils places the oldest specimens some 195,000 years ago in Africa. New genetic studies based on mitochondrial DNA have corroborated that date and have also contributed to determining the possible migration routes that permitted the slow expansion of *H. sapiens* to other continents. Meanwhile, the new discoveries raise unanswered questions about what happened in the course of the 150,000 years that preceded the great cultural revolution that characterizes *H. sapiens* and that occurred some 40,000 years ago with the appearance of Cro-Magnon in Europe. ●

Homo sapiens sapiens

It is believed that Cro-Magnon arrived in Europe some 40,000 years ago. Evidence of prehistoric art, symbolism, and ritual ceremonies distinguish this advanced culture from other species of hominins that preceded it. It was well-adapted to its environment, lived in caves, and developed techniques of hunting in groups. It captured large animals with traps and small ones with rocks.

TOOLS
Homo sapiens invented multiple tools for various uses and were usually made from stone, bone, horns, and wood.

EVOLUTION OF THE SKULL
Cro-Magnon had a small face, high forehead, and longer chin.

CRANIAL CAPACITY
Its cranial cavity could hold a brain of up to 97 cubic inches (1,590 cu cm).

150,000 YEARS AGO

120,000 YEARS AGO

The "Mitochondrial Eve" is the common ancestor of all people.

Homo sapiens begins to extend through Africa.

Theories of Expansion

There is no agreement among scientists about how the expansion of *Homo sapiens* to the entire world took place. It is believed that the "Mitochondrial Eve," the most recent common ancestor, lived in Africa, because the people of that continent have greater genetic diversity than those of the other continents. From there, in various migratory waves, *Homo sapiens* would have reached Asia, Australia, and Europe. However, some scientists think that there were no such migrations but that modern humans evolved more or less simultaneously in various regions of the ancient world.

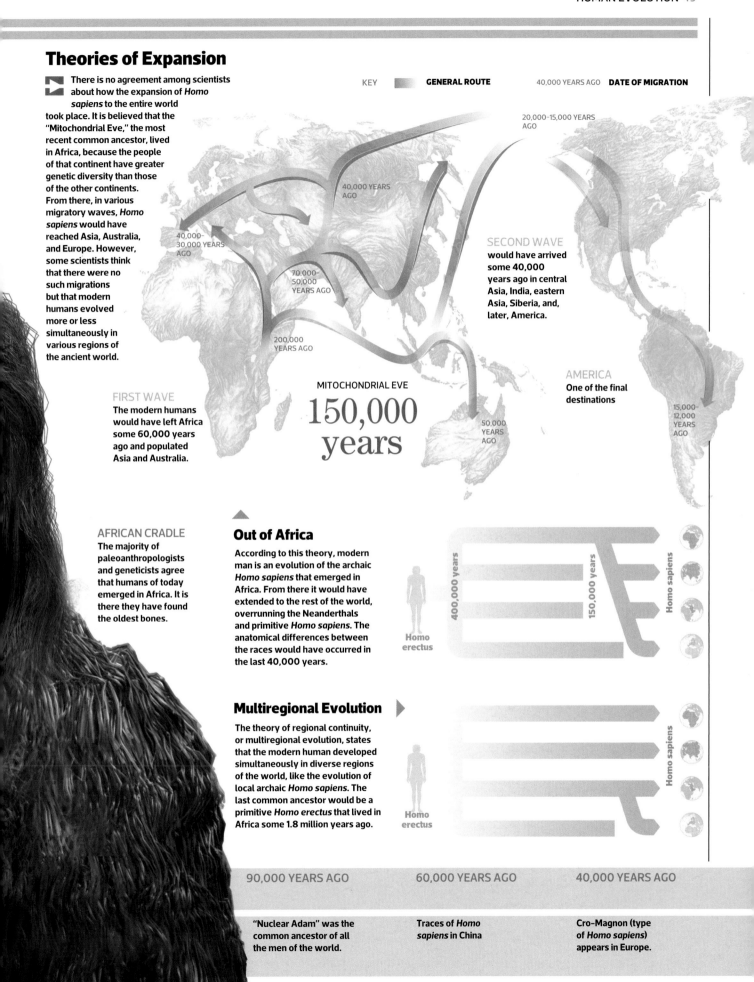

KEY · **GENERAL ROUTE** · 40,000 YEARS AGO **DATE OF MIGRATION**

20,000-15,000 YEARS AGO

40,000 YEARS AGO

40,000-30,000 YEARS AGO

70,000-50,000 YEARS AGO

200,000 YEARS AGO

SECOND WAVE
would have arrived some 40,000 years ago in central Asia, India, eastern Asia, Siberia, and, later, America.

AMERICA
One of the final destinations

15,000-12,000 YEARS AGO

MITOCHONDRIAL EVE

150,000 years

50,000 YEARS AGO

FIRST WAVE
The modern humans would have left Africa some 60,000 years ago and populated Asia and Australia.

AFRICAN CRADLE
The majority of paleoanthropologists and geneticists agree that humans of today emerged in Africa. It is there they have found the oldest bones.

Out of Africa

According to this theory, modern man is an evolution of the archaic *Homo sapiens* that emerged in Africa. From there it would have extended to the rest of the world, overrunning the Neanderthals and primitive *Homo sapiens*. The anatomical differences between the races would have occurred in the last 40,000 years.

400,000 years · *Homo erectus* · 150,000 years · *Homo sapiens*

Multiregional Evolution

The theory of regional continuity, or multiregional evolution, states that the modern human developed simultaneously in diverse regions of the world, like the evolution of local archaic *Homo sapiens*. The last common ancestor would be a primitive *Homo erectus* that lived in Africa some 1.8 million years ago.

Homo erectus · *Homo sapiens*

90,000 YEARS AGO	60,000 YEARS AGO	40,000 YEARS AGO
"Nuclear Adam" was the common ancestor of all the men of the world.	Traces of *Homo sapiens* in China	Cro-Magnon (type of *Homo sapiens*) appears in Europe.

Culture, the Great Leap

Although questions remain about how culture originated, it is almost impossible to determine which things of the human world are natural and which are not. Scientists of many disciplines are trying to answer these questions from the evidence of prehistoric life found by paleontologists. The subspecies of mammals to which man belongs, *Homo sapiens sapiens,* appeared in Africa some 150,000 years ago, disseminated through the entire Old World some 30,000 years ago (date that the oldest signs of art were found), and colonized America 11,000 years ago; but the first traces of agriculture, industry, population centers, and control over nature date from barely the last 10,000 years. Some believe that the definitive leap toward culture was achieved through the acquisition of a creative language capable of expressing ideas and sentiments more advanced than the simple communication of *Homo erectus.* ●

The first artists

Cave paintings, like those of the caves of Altamira (Spain) and Lascaux (France), leave no doubt that those who made them truly possessed the attributes of human beings. Architecture had not arrived, but paintings had, engraved and sculptured in stone or bone. There exist various theories about the function of cave painting that consider the aesthetic, the magical, the social, and the religious—not much different from the questions about art today.

CAVE-PAINTING TECHNIQUES

GEOMETRIC DESIGNS
Dotted and lineal geometric designs, along with mythical chimeras, have been found among European cave paintings similar to the rock art of Aboriginal Australians.

BLOWING
One technique consisted of blowing pigment through a rod or hollow bone.

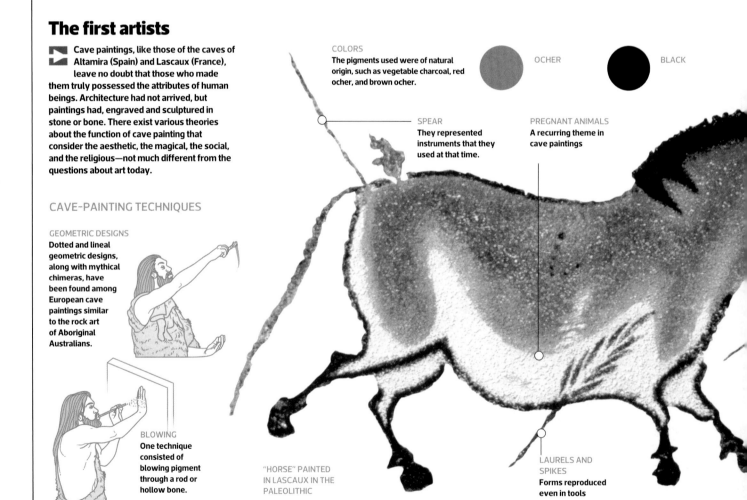

COLORS
The pigments used were of natural origin, such as vegetable charcoal, red ocher, and brown ocher.

OCHER

BLACK

SPEAR
They represented instruments that they used at that time.

PREGNANT ANIMALS
A recurring theme in cave paintings

"HORSE" PAINTED IN LASCAUX IN THE PALEOLITHIC

LAURELS AND SPIKES
Forms reproduced even in tools

WÜRM GLACIATION 35,000 YEARS	AURIGNACIAN 30,000 YEARS AGO	PERIGORDIAN 27,000 YEARS AGO
The Upper Paleolithic begins.	Tools of mammoth tusk, flake tools	Well-cut tools, including a multiangle graver

ART ON THE WALLS

Cave painting is a phenomenon that was found mainly in the current regions of France and Spain. In France, there are more than 130 caves; the most famous are located in the Aquitaine region (Lascaux, Pech-Merle, Laugerie, La Madeleine) and in the Pyrenees (Niaux, Le Tucs d'Audubert, Bedeilhac). Spain has some 60 caves in the Cantabria region to the north, among them the cave of Altamira, and 180 caves farther south. Examples from other regions include caves at Addaura, Italy, and Kapova, Russia. Portable art, on the other hand, was abundant in all Europe.

EUROPE

Sites in Europe where Paleolithic art has been found

BLACK SEA

MEDITERRANEAN SEA

14,000
years old
THE PAINTINGS OF ALTAMIRA

MICROCEPHALY
The head is small in relation to the rest of the animal's body.

Builders of objects

Homo sapiens sapiens distinguished itself from its ancestors, who were already making rudimentary tools, through the growing use of such new materials as bone and above all for the specialization of new tools. Mortars, knives, boring tools, and axes had forms and functions continually more sophisticated. There also appeared, in addition to utensils and tools, objects with ornamental and representative functions that attested to humans' increasing capacity for symbolism. These manifestations, through which the art could leave the caves, are known as portable art. It produced objects that were utilitarian, luxurious, or ceremonial, like the Paleolithic "Venus" figurines.

SYMBOLISM
The "Venus of Willendorf" measures 4 inches (11 cm) in height and was found in Austria.

24,000
years old
IS THE AGE OF THIS LITTLE STATUE

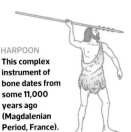

OTHER THEMES AND MOTIVES

PALEOLITHIC TOOLS

HUNTING SCENES IN THE CAVE OF TASSILI-N-AJJER, ALGERIA

HANDS IMPRINTED AS A NEGATIVE APPEAR IN MULTIPLE PLACES.

TWO-SIDED KNIFE
Its invention presaged the most important cultural revolution of the Upper Paleolithic.

HARPOON
This complex instrument of bone dates from some 11,000 years ago (Magdalenian Period, France).

POLISHED AX
Found in Wetzlar, Germany, it shows the polishing technique of 20,000 years ago.

SOLUTREAN
20,000-50,000 YEARS AGO

Use of oxide to paint, pointed instruments

MAGDALENIAN
15,000 YEARS AGO

The greatest flourishing of cave art in southern Europe

END OF PALEOLITHIC
9,000 BC

End of the glaciations, with an improvement of the global climate

Urban Revolution

Some 10,000 years ago, there was an interglacial period on Earth that caused a gradual increase in temperatures and an overall climatic change that brought a modification to the life of humans. Instead of roaming from place to place to hunt, people began to create societies based on sedentary life, agriculture, and the domestication of animals. Some villages grew so much that they became true cities, such as Çatal Hüyük in southern Turkey. In the ruins of this city, considered one of the milestones of modern archaeology, were found a good number of ceramics and statues of the so-called mother goddess—a woman giving birth—that belonged to a fertility ritual. In addition, there are signs that the inhabitants practiced funeral rights and built dolmens for collective graves. ●

CITY OF
ÇATAL HÜYÜK

The Neolithic City of Çatal Hüyük

Çatal Hüyük is located in southern Anatolia (Turkey). Houses were built side by side, sharing a common wall. There were no exterior windows or openings, and the buildings had flat-terraced roofs. People entered through the roof, and there were usually one or two stories. The walls and terraces were made of plaster and then painted red. In some main residences, there were paintings on the walls and roof. The houses were made of mud bricks and had a sanctuary dedicated to the mother goddess. During the excavation, many religious articles were uncovered: the majority were ceramic figures in relief depicting the mother goddess and heads of bulls and leopards.

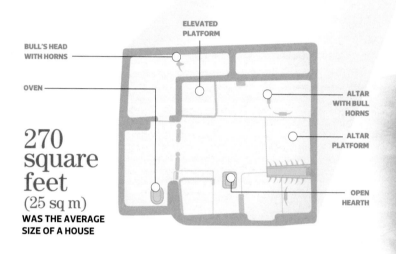

BULL'S HEAD
WITH HORNS

OVEN

ELEVATED
PLATFORM

ALTAR
WITH BULL
HORNS

ALTAR
PLATFORM

OPEN
HEARTH

270 square feet
(25 sq m)
WAS THE AVERAGE SIZE OF A HOUSE

OTHER TYPES OF CONSTRUCTION
The process of carrying out a megalithic construction began in a quarry, where large blocks of stone were extracted.

1 Transport
The stones were transported on rollers to the place chosen for the erection of the monument.

2 Erection
The blocks were dropped into a hole and placed in a vertical position.

3 Earthworks
Embankments were made for the construction of a dolmen.

4 Trilith
The horizontal block was transported over an embankment and placed on the two upright stones.

8000 BC

7000 BC

6000 BC

First indications of agricultural activities

Expansion of agriculture.
Complex funerary rites.

Stable settlements in the Persian Gulf

CROPS

In the fields near Çatal Hüyük, the inhabitants grew wheat, sorghum, peas, and lentils. They gathered apples, pistachios, and almonds.

LENTILS

APPLES

WHEAT

6,000
years BC
ÇATAL HÜYÜK
WAS ONE OF THE
FIRST CITIES.

LOCATION OF ÇATAL HÜYÜK

Country	Turkey
Year	7000 BC
Type of City	Farming–livestock

MOTHER
GODDESS

CULTS

There is a direct relationship between the emergence of agriculture and the cult of the feminine because of the importance of fertility. Statuettes of pregnant women were found in homes in shrines decorated with molded bull heads and other figures.

3500 BC

AD 320

Invention of writing in Mesopotamia

First vehicles with wheels in Asia

Mechanisms of Heredity

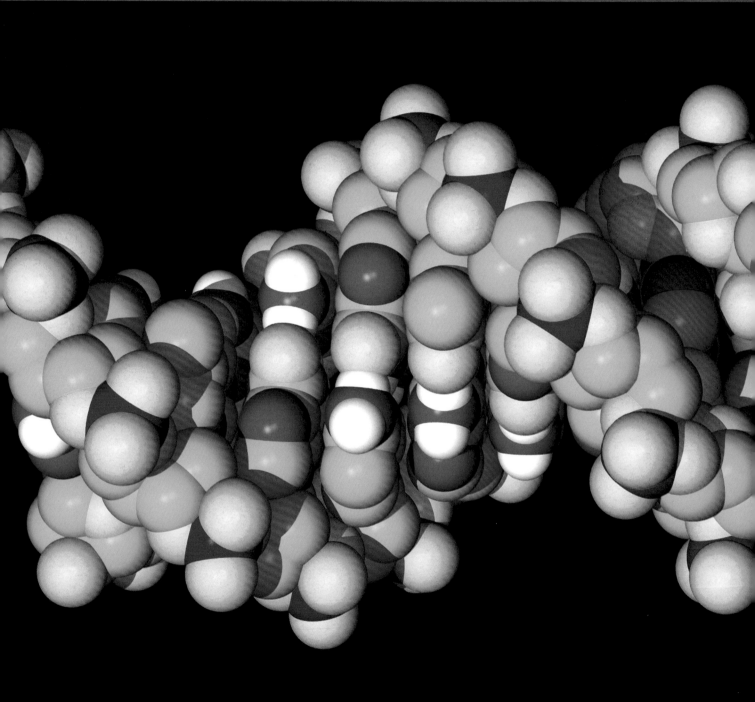

The cells of the body are constantly dividing to replace damaged cells. Before a cell divides to create new cells, a process known as mitosis, or to form ovules or spermatozoa, a process called meiosis, the DNA included in each cell needs to copy, or replicate, itself. This process is possible because the DNA strands

DNA
Complex macromolecule
that contains a chemical
code for all the information
necessary for life

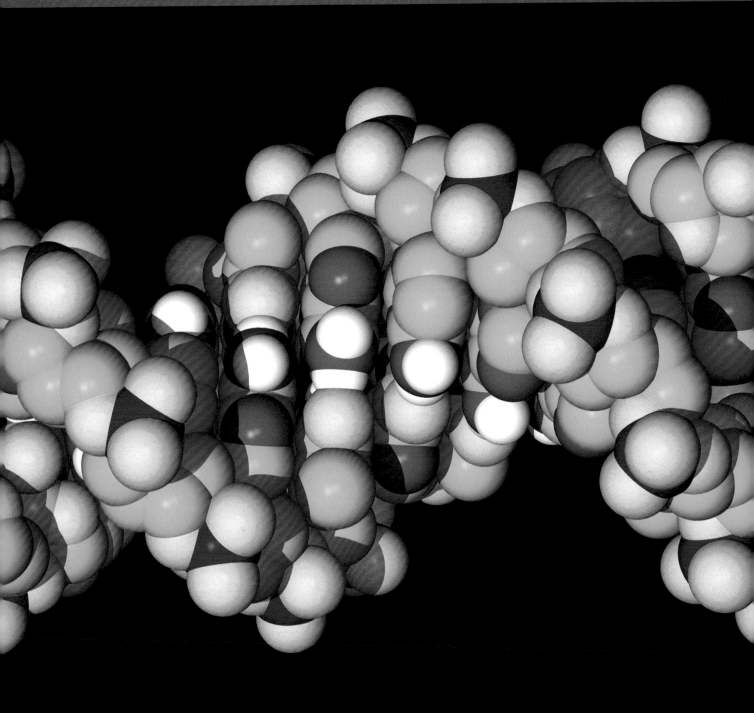

can open and separate. Each of the two strands of the original DNA serves as a model for a new strand. In this chapter, we will also tell you how human beings vary in height, weight, skin color, eyes, and other physical characteristics despite belonging to the same species. The secret is in the genes, and we will show it to you in a simple way. ●

Self-Copying

All living organisms utilize cellular division as a mechanism for reproduction or growth. The cellular cycle has a phase called the S phase in which the duplication of the hereditary material, or DNA, occurs. In this phase, two identical sister chromatids are united into one chromosome. Once this phase of duplication is finalized, the original and the duplicate will form the structures necessary for mitosis and, in addition, give a signal for the whole process of cellular division to start.

The Cellular Nucleus

The nucleus is the control center of the cell. Generally it is the most noticeable structure of the cell. Within it are found the chromosomes, which are formed by DNA. In human beings, each cellular nucleus is composed of 23 pairs of chromosomes. The nucleus is surrounded by a porous membrane made up of two layers.

GROWTH AND CELLULAR DIVISION

The cellular cycle includes cell growth, in which the cell increases in mass and duplicates its organelles, and cell division, in which DNA is replicated and the nuclei divide.

1

PHASE G1
The cell doubles in size. The number of organelles, enzymes, and other molecules increases.

INTERPHASE

5

CYTOKINESIS
The cytoplasm of the mother cell divides and gives rise to two daughter cells identical to the mother.

4

MITOSIS
The two sets of chromosomes are distributed, one set for each nucleus of the two daughter cells.

6.5 feet
(2 m)
**LENGTH OF DNA
IN HUMAN CELL
CHROMOSOMES**

HOW THEY LOOK

Once they have duplicated, the
chromosomes form a structure
in the shape of a cross. In this
structure, the centromere functions as
the point of union for the chromatids.

History of
the Chromosome

The chromosomes carry the genetic information
that controls the characteristics of a human
being, which are passed from the parents to the
children and from generation to generation. They were
discovered by Karl Wilhelm von Nägeli in 1842. In 1910
Thomas Hunt Morgan discovered the primordial function
of the chromosomes: he called them carriers of genes.
Thanks to demonstrating this, Morgan received the Nobel
Prize for Physiology or Medicine in 1933.

46
chromosomes
HUMAN BEING

AMOUNT OF
CHROMOSOMES
ACCORDING TO SPECIES

The number of chromosomes of
a species varies independently
of its size and complexity. A fern
has thousands of chromosomes
and a fly only a few pairs.

24
chromosomes
SALAMANDER

1,262
chromosomes
FERNS

2

S PHASE
The DNA and associated
proteins are copied,
resulting in two copies of
the genetic information.

8
chromosomes
FRUIT FLY

3

PHASE G2
The chromosomes begin
to condense. The cell
prepares for division.

The Chromosome

The chromosome is a structural unit that consists of a molecule of DNA associated with proteins. Eukaryote chromosomes condense during mitosis and meiosis and form structures visible through a microscope. They are made of DNA (deoxyribonucleic acid), RNA (ribonucleic acid), and proteins. The majority of the proteins are histones, small positively charged molecules. Chromosomes carry the genes, the functional structures responsible for the characteristics of each individual.

Karyotype

The ordering and systematic classification of the chromosomes by pairs, size, and position of the centromere. The chromosomes that are seen in a karyotype are found in the metaphase of mitosis. Each one of them consists of two sister chromatids united by their centromeres.

1

CHROMATINS
There are two types: euchromatin, lightly packed, and heterochromatin, more densely packed. The majority of nuclear chromatin consists of euchromatin.

30 rosettes
IN EACH TURN OF THE SPIRAL

Carrier of Genes

In the DNA, certain segments of the molecule are called genes. These segments have the genetic information that will determine the characteristics of an individual or will permit the synthesis of a certain protein. The information necessary for generating the entire organism is found in each cell, but only the part of the information necessary for reproducing this specific type of cell is activated. The reading and transmission of the information for use outside the nucleus is performed by messenger RNA.

PROKARYOTE CELL
Prokaryote cells do not have a cellular nucleus, so the DNA is found in the cytoplasm. The size of the DNA differs according to species. Prokaryotes are almost all unicellular organisms

2

THE FRAMEWORK

Each one of the rosettes consists of loops stabilized by the "scaffolding" of other proteins. These loops help to condense the chromatin.

6
loops
IN EACH ROSETTE

3

SOLENOID

A group of six nucleosomes that form each turn inside the loops

0.0000012 inch
(0.00003 mm)

DIAMETER OF EACH SOLENOID

6
nucleosomes
IN EACH TURN

PEARL NECKLACE

If the DNA chain is stretched and observed under a microscope, it resembles beads on a string. Nevertheless, DNA chains are generally found pressed very tightly around the nucleus.

SPACER DNA

The nucleosomes are united by chains of base pairs of DNA 0.0000004 inch (0.00001 mm) long.

60
base pairs
THE AMOUNT OF DNA BETWEEN NUCLEOSOMES

NITROGEN BASES

CIRCULAR CHROMOSOME OF BACTERIA

4

NUCLEOSOME

A group of eight histone molecules with two DNA spirals twisted around them. The "tails" of the histones seem to interact with the molecules that regulate genetic activity.

The Replication of Life

n deoxyribonucleic acid—DNA—all the genetic information of a complete organism is found. It has complete control of heredity. A DNA molecule consists of two strands of relatively simple compounds called nucleotides. Each nucleotide consists of a phosphate, sugar, and one of four kinds of nitrogenous bases. The nucleotides on each strand are paired in specific combinations and connected to each other by hydrogen bonds. The two strands coil around each other in the form of a spiral, or double helix.

NEW CHAIN

REPLICATION

The genetic information is encoded in the sequence of the bases of the DNA nucleotides aligned along the DNA molecule. The specificity of the pairing of these bases is the key to the replication of DNA. There are only two possible combinations—thymine with adenine and guanine with cytosine—to form the complementary links of the strands that make up the DNA chain.

Complementary

Various specialized proteins called enzymes act as biological catalysts, accelerating the reactions of replication: helicase, which is in charge of opening the double helix of DNA; polymerase, which is in charge of synthesizing the new strands of DNA in one direction; and ligase, which seals and joins the fragments of DNA that were synthesized.

50 nucleotides
PER SECOND IS THE SPEED OF DNA REPLICATION IN HUMANS.

ORIGINAL CHAIN

Biological Revolution

Deciphering the molecular structure of DNA was the major triumph of biomolecular studies in biology. Based on work by Rosalind Franklin on the diffraction of X-rays by DNA, James Watson and Francis Crick demonstrated the double-helix composition of DNA in 1953 and for their work won the 1962 Nobel Prize for Physiology or Medicine.

① WEAK BRIDGES

Helicase separates the double helix, thus initiating the replication of both chains. The chains serve as a model to make a new double helix.

② FREED ENERGY

The energy to form new links is obtained from the phosphate groups. The free nitrogenous bases are found in the form of triphosphates. The separation of the phosphates provides the energy to interlace the nucleotides in the new chain that is being built.

③ NEW CONNECTION

The new chains of DNA couple in short segments, and the ligase joins them to form the daughter molecules.

④ PERFECT REPLICATION

The result is two new molecules, each with one strand from the original DNA and one new complementary strand. This is called semiconservative replication. The genetic information of the new strand is identical to that of the original DNA molecule.

COPY

ORIGINAL

BASIC MECHANISM

The new bases join to make a DNA chain that is a daughter of the previous model.

GUANINE

ADENINE

HYDROGEN BOND

CYTOSINE

THYMINE

Nucleotides

The nucleotides have three subunits: a phosphate group, a five-carbon sugar, and a nitrogenous base. In DNA these bases are small organic molecules. Adenine and guanine are purines, and cytosine and thymine are pyrimidines, smaller than the purines. All are composed of nitrogen, hydrogen, carbon, and oxygen—except for adenine, which has no oxygen. The adenine is always paired with thymine and guanine with cytosine. The first pair is joined by two hydrogen bonds and the second by three.

DNA TRANSCRIPTION

The process of copying one simple chain of DNA is called transcription. For it to happen, the double strands separate through the action of an enzyme, permitting the enzyme RNA polymerase to connect to one of the strands. Then, using the DNA strand as a model, the enzyme begins synthesizing messenger RNA from the free nitrogenous bases that are found inside the nucleus.

1

SEPARATION OF DNA
When the DNA is to be transcribed, its double chain separates, leaving a sequence of DNA bases free to be newly matched.

2

TRANSCRIPTION
One of the chains, called the transcriptor, is replicated by the addition of free bases in the nucleus through the action of an enzyme called RNA polymerase. The result is a simple chain of mRNA (messenger RNA).

30
bases per second
ARE COPIED DURING THE PROCESS OF TRANSCRIPTION.

Transcription of the Genetic Code

This complex process of translation allows the information stored in nuclear DNA to arrive at the organelles of the cell to conduct the synthesis of polypeptides. RNA (ribonucleic acid) is key to this process. The mRNA (messenger RNA) is in charge of carrying information transcribed from the nucleus as a simple chain of bases to the ribosome. The ribosome, together with transfer RNA (tRNA), translates the mRNA and assembles surrounding amino acids following the genetic instructions.

COMPRESSION OF RNA
In the formation of mRNA, useless parts are eliminated to reduce its size.

— With introns

Without introns

DNA RNA MATURE RNA

SYNTHESIS OF POLYPEPTIDES

The polypeptides form when a group of amino acids unite in a chain. For this to happen, the ribosome: translates the information that the mRNA transcribed from the nuclear DNA; codifies the amino acids and their order with the help of tRNA, through the matching of codons and anticodons; and places each amino acid exactly where it belongs.

RIBOSOME

The cellular organelle where the synthesis of polypeptides occurs. It helps translate the information brought by the mRNA.

ENZYMES

collaborate in the formation of the polypeptide chain by making the peptide chains that join the amino acids.

tRNA

Transfer RNA is in charge of recognizing and translating the information that the mRNA contains.

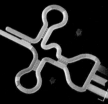

ANTICODON

POLYPEPTIDES

are formations of about 10 to 50 amino acids. Each amino acid is considered a peptide.

5 INTERRUPTION

The synthesis is produced between the start codon and the stop codon. Once the chain reaches the stopping point, the ribosome stops synthesizing the polypeptide, and the ribosome releases the polypeptide.

3 LEAVING THE NUCLEUS

If the DNA were to leave the nucleus, it would get corrupted, so it is the mRNA that transcribes the DNA's information in a simple chain, which takes the information to the cytoplasm of the cell.

4 TRANSLATION

In the ribosome the translation of the mRNA to synthesize the polypeptide is initiated with the participation of tRNA.

The Path of the Gene

Sexual differences in the heredity of traits constitute a model known as sex-linked inheritance. The father of genetics was Gregor Mendel. He established the principle of independent segregation, which is possible only when the genes are situated on different chromosomes; if the genes are found on the same chromosome, they are linked, tending to be inherited together. Later Thomas Morgan contributed more evidence of sex-linked inheritance. Today many traits are identified in this model, such as hemophilia and color blindness. ●

3
ANAPHASE I
The chiasmata separate. The chromosomes separate from their homologues to incorporate themselves into the nucleus of the daughter cell.

A **MEIOSIS I**

This first division has four phases, of which prophase 1 is the most characteristic of meiosis, since it encompasses its fundamental processes—pairing and crossing over, which allow the number of chromosomes by the end of this process to be reduced by half.

2
METAPHASE I
The nuclear membrane disappears. The chiasmata, composed of two chromosomes, align, and the centromeres move away.

21

PROPHASE I
The homologous chromosomes pair up, forming chiasmata, which are unique to meiosis.

■ CHROMOSOME FROM THE MOTHER

■ CHROMOSOME FROM THE FATHER

Linkage
The genes, arranged in linear form and on the same chromosome, are inherited as isolated units.

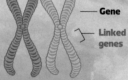

Gene

Linked genes

A CHROMOSOMES DIFFERENTIATED BY THEIR GENES

Crossing Over
Process in which a pair of analogous chromosomes exchange material while they are joined

B INFORMATION CROSSING OVER

C RESULTING PAIR OF CHROMOSOMES

D POSSIBLE COMBINATIONS

CENTROMERE

4

TELOPHASE I

The nuclear membranes reform, and the number of chromosomes enclosed in each has been reduced by half.

5

PROPHASE II

The division of the new daughter cells begins: the chromatids condense; the nuclear membranes disintegrate; and the spindles form.

B **MEIOSIS II**

In the second division, the two chromatids that form each chromosome from meiosis I are separated. As a result of this double division, four daughter cells are produced that contain half the characteristic chromosomal number—i.e., 23 chromosomes each (haploid cells). Each chromosome will be composed of a chromatid.

6

METAPHASE II

continues in the daughter cells. The chromosomes align at their middle, and the chromatids affix themselves to the fibers of the spindle.

7

ANAPHASE II

The centromeres divide again, and the sister chromatids divide, going to opposite poles.

HEREDITY

In human beings, some genes have been identified that are found in the heterochromosomes and deal with sex linkage. For example, the genes that code for hemophilia and color blindness are found in the heterochromosome X.

Gregor Mendel

(1822–84)

POSTULATED THE FIRST LAWS OF INHERITANCE.

8

NUCLEUS OF TELOPHASE

The spindle disappears and forms a membrane around each nucleus.

9

NEW NUCLEI

The new formations have a haploid endowment of chromosomes.

10

CYTOKINESIS

The cytoplasm divides, separating the mother cell into two daughter cells.

1920

THOMAS MORGAN studied the color of eyes in the fly *Drosophilia melangaster*.

Problems of Heredity

Toward the end of the 19th century, the form in which the physical traits of parents were transmitted to their offspring was uncertain. This uncertainty extended to the breeding of plants and animals, which posed a problem for agriculture and livestock producers. In their fields they sowed plants and raised animals without knowing what the quality of their products would be. The work of Gregor Mendel and his contributions to molecular genetics eventually led to a solution to these problems and to an understanding of how the mechanisms of heredity work. ●

The legacy of Mendel

 The principles proposed by Mendel are the basis of classical, or Mendelian, genetics, which reached its peak at the beginning of the 20th century. This science studies how the variants, or alleles, for a morphological trait are transmitted from one generation to the next. Later, after confirmation that the components of the nucleus are those in charge of controlling heredity, molecular genetics developed. This science studies heredity on a molecular level and analyzes how the structure of DNA and its functional units, or genes, are responsible for heredity. Molecular genetics links classical genetics and molecular biology. Its use allows us to know the relationship that exists between visible traits and the molecular hereditary information.

DOMINANT AND RECESSIVE

The traits of a gene in an individual are expressed according to a pair of variants, or alleles. In general, the dominant alleles are expressed even though there may be another allele for the same gene. A recessive allele is expressed only if it is the only allele present in the pair.

DOMINANT
With two dominant alleles, the individual is homozygous dominant for this trait.

HETEROZYGOUS
When there is an allele of each type, the individual is heterozygous for this trait.

HOMOZYGOUS
With two recessive alleles, the individual is homozygous recessive for this trait.

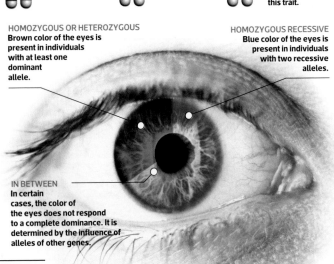

HOMOZYGOUS OR HETEROZYGOUS
Brown color of the eyes is present in individuals with at least one dominant allele.

HOMOZYGOUS RECESSIVE
Blue color of the eyes is present in individuals with two recessive alleles.

IN BETWEEN
In certain cases, the color of the eyes does not respond to a complete dominance. It is determined by the influence of alleles of other genes.

FROM THE GARDEN

During the 19th century, the gardens of the Abbey of Saint Thomas were the laboratory that Mendel used for his experiments on heredity. During the 20th century, classical genetics and molecular genetics amplified our knowledge about the mechanism of heredity.

1869
The Austrian Augustinian monk Gregor Mendel proposes the laws that explain the mechanisms of heredity. His proposal is ignored by scientists.

1869
Johann Friedrich Miescher, a Swiss doctor, suggests that deoxyribonucleic acid, or DNA, is responsible for the transmission of hereditary traits.

1889
Wilhelm von Waldeyer gives the name "chromosomes" to the structures that form cellular DNA.

1900
The German Carl Erich Correns, the Austrian Erich Tschermak, and the Dutchman Hugo de Vries discover, independently, the works of Mendel.

1926
T.H. Morgan demonstrates that the genes are found united in different groups of linkages in the chromosomes.

1953
James Watson and Francis Crick propose a double-helix polymer model for the structure of DNA.

1973
Investigators produce the first genetically modified bacteria.

1977
North American scientists for the first time introduce genetic material from human cells into bacteria.

1982
The United States commercializes recombinant insulin produced by means of genetic engineering.

1990
An international public consortium initiates the project to decipher the human genome.

1997
Dolly the sheep is the first cloned mammal.

2000
The Human Genome Project and the company Celera publish the deciphered human genome.

The man who calculated

Gregor Johann Mendel was born in Heinzendorf, Austria, in 1822 and died in the city of Brünn, Austria–Hungary (now Brno, Czech Republic) in 1884. He was a monk of the Augustinian order who at the University of Vienna pursued, over three years, different studies in mathematics, physics, and natural sciences. This ample academic training and his great intellectual capacity permitted him to develop a series of experiments in which he used pea plants (*Pisum sativum*). He analyzed various traits, among them the appearance of flowers, fruits, stems, and leaves. In his methodology, he included an innovation: he submitted his results to mathematical calculations. His conclusions were key to understanding the mechanism of heredity.

PEAS The pea plants of the *Pisum sativum* species were key for the conclusions obtained by Mendel about heredity.

BOTANY This display is a botanical teaching tool. An altruistic naturalist, Mendel dedicated himself to conserving in herbariums the specimens of different species of plants.

Uniformity

P

Mendel's first law, or principle, about heredity proposes that by crossing two homozygous parents (P), dominant and recessive for the same trait, its descendant, or filial 1 (F_1), will be uniform. That is, all those F1 individuals will be identical for the homozygous dominant trait. In this example using the trait seed color, yellow is dominant and green is recessive. Thus, the F_1 generation will be yellow.

PURE INDIVIDUALS

1 Mendel used pure individuals, plants that he knew were homozygous dominant and recessive for a specific trait. For his experiments, Mendel carefully covered or directly cut the stamens of the flowers to prevent them from self-fertilizing.

Traits and Alleles

P

The first law, known as the law of segregation, comes from the results obtained with the crosses made with F_1 individuals. At the reappearance of the color green in the descendants, or filial 2 (F_2) generation, he deduced that the trait seed color is represented through variants, or alleles, that code for yellow (dominant color) and green (recessive color).

Independence

The second law, called the law of independent assortment, proposes that the alleles of different traits are transmitted independently to the descendant. This can be demonstrated by analyzing the results of the experiments in which Mendel examined simultaneously the heredity of two traits. For example, he analyzed the traits "color and surface texture of seeds." He took as dominant alleles those for yellow and a smooth surface and as recessive the alleles for green and a wrinkled surface. Later he crossed pure plants with both characteristics and obtained the F_1 generation that exhibited only dominant alleles. The self-fertilization of the F_1 generation produced F_2 individuals in the constant proportion 9:3:3:1, showing that combinations of alleles were transmitted in an independent manner.

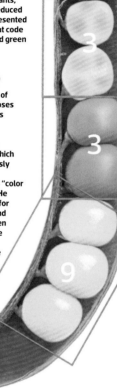

1
3
3
9

Yellow

CROSSING

F_1

OBTAINING THE FIRST FILIAL GENERATION

Yellow

Yellow: 3 Green: 1

The cross, or self-fertilization, of individuals of the F_1 generation produces F_2 individuals with yellow and green seeds in constant 3:1 ratio. In addition, it is deduced that the F_1 generation is made up of heterozygous individuals.

Green

Yellow

SELF-FERTILIZATION

F_2

OBTAINING THE SECOND FILIAL GENERATION

INSEMINATION

2 Once self-fertilization was impeded, Mendel inseminated the pollen of a homozygous dominant on an ovary of a homozygous recessive and vice versa. In addition to color, he analyzed other traits, such as length of stem, appearance of seeds, and color of flowers.

TALL STEM

SHORT STEM

FRUITFUL WORK

3 When the plants produced legumes, the seeds exhibited determined colors. Upon carrying out his experiments on hundreds of individuals, he obtained much information. The monk recorded the data in tables and submitted them to probability analysis. In this way Mendel synthesized his results into the conclusions that we know today as the Mendelian laws, or principles, of inheritance.

GREEN The green seeds appear in lower proportion than the yellow.

The Age of Genetics

DNA ANALYSIS
Genetic identification is a nearly infallible proof of identity used in cases of disappearance, rape, murder, and paternity suits.

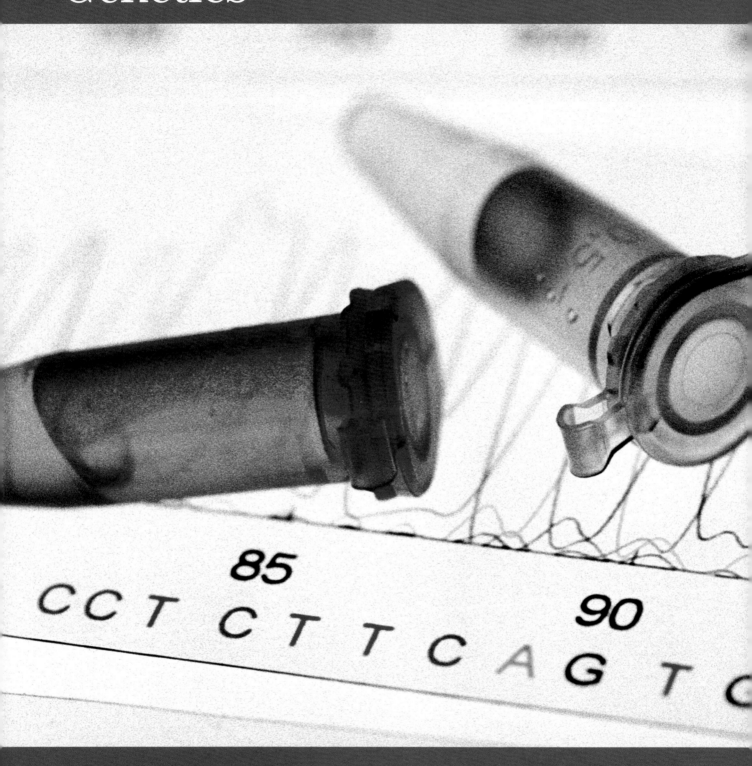

85

CCT CTTCAGTG

90

D NA analysis has become a common practice in diagnosing and predicting genetically inherited diseases. It is also highly useful in forensic procedures. The DNA sequence, like fingerprints, is unique to each individual. In these pages you will learn about achievements in the field of genetically modified foods

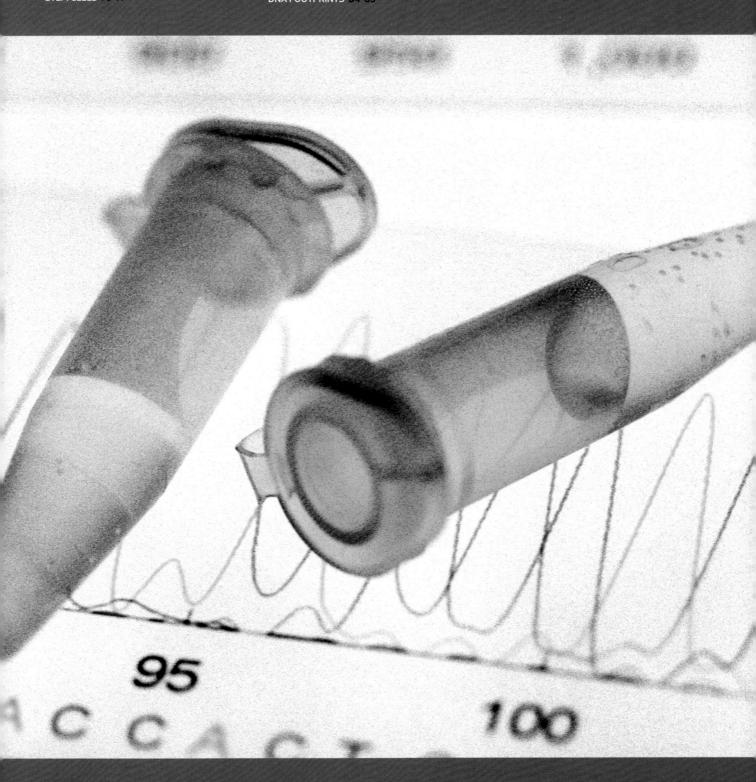

and animals, the latest advances in genetic medicine, and future applications of stem cells. According to specialists, these cells could be used to regenerate damaged tissues or organs. Another technique that will surely provide a definitive cure for serious diseases will involve exchanging defective genes for healthy ones. ●

Genetic Solution

G enetic engineering applies technologies for manipulating and transferring DNA between separate organisms. It enables the improvement of animal and plant species, the correction of defective genes, and the production of many useful compounds. For example, some microorganisms are genetically modified to manufacture human proteins, which are vital for those who do not produce them efficiently. ●

Genetic Engineering

Genetic recombination consists of integrating DNA from different organisms. For example, a plasmid is used to insert a known portion of human DNA into the DNA of bacteria. The bacteria then incorporate new genetic information into their chromosomes. When their own DNA is transcribed, the new DNA is transcribed as well. Thus, the bacteria formulate both their own proteins and foreign proteins, such as human insulin.

① Extraction

DNA is extracted from a human cell to obtain the gene that codes for producing insulin. The DNA is cut using restriction enzymes that recognize the points where the gene in question begins and ends. These enzymes also cut the bacterial plasmid. The DNA fragments thus obtained have irregular and complementary ends.

② Union

The human and bacterial DNA join at their free ends and form a recombined plasmid. This plasmid contains the human insulin gene.

③ Insertion

A culture of nonpathogenic receptor bacteria is placed in a solution that contains the recombined plasmid. The solution is then subjected to chemical and electrical stimuli to incorporate the plasmid that contains the insulin gene.

RECOMBINANT DNA
The recombined plasmid is inserted into the receptor bacteria.

RECOMBINED PLASMID WITH HUMAN DNA

EXTRA DNA
The plasmids may contain up to 250,000 nitrogenous bases outside the chromosome.

ROUND CHROMOSOME

BACTERIAL PLASMID

BACTERIA
***Escherichia coli* contain plasmids (DNA molecules that are separate from chromosomal DNA).**

INSULIN GENE
The DNA sequences for producing insulin are inserted separately into different plasmids.

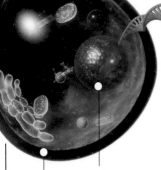

NUCLEUS

HUMAN CELL
Each body cell has genetic information.

BACTERIAL PLASMID

MODEL ORGANISMS
Besides *E. coli*, eukaryote cells such as yeast are used.

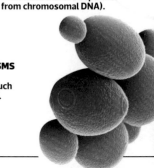

10 HOURS
are needed for the culture population to double.

INSERTION INTO THE CHROMOSOME
The recombined plasmid is inserted into the bacteria's chromosome.

BACTERIA
In phase of exponential growth. From now on, they will produce the hormone insulin.

Reproduction
The bacteria reproduce constantly in fermentation tanks with water and essential nutrients. In these conditions, the recombined bacteria transcribe the information in their chromosomes to produce proteins. The bacteria also read the information from the human DNA that was inserted using the recombined plasmid, and they produce insulin.

NEW INSULIN
The transcription of human DNA enables the formation of recombined human insulin.

HIGH PRESSURE

TINY TUBE

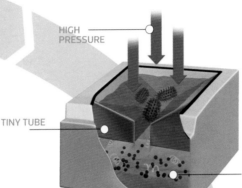

⑤ Purification
The culture is circulated at high pressure through tiny tubes that destroy the bacteria. The solution contains a large amount of insulin that must be separated from the other proteins in the solution.

CELLULAR REMAINS

INSULIN

First Case
Insulin was the first protein produced by genetic engineering. It was approved for human use in 1982.

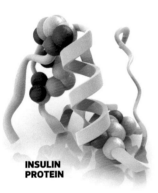

INSULIN PROTEIN

CENTRIFUGAL FORCE
Centrifugal force accelerates the decantation.

GLASS TUBES

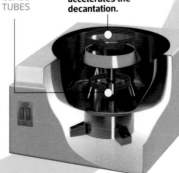

⑥ Centrifugation
Centrifuges separate the various compounds present in the solution from the bacterial remains and the human insulin. The proteins present in the solid matter are separated from the original solution.

BEFORE CENTRIFUGATION

AFTER CENTRIFUGATION

The separated material that contains bacterial remains.

Insulin in bacterial batch

Insulin pellet

DECANTATION
The centrifuges reduce the amount of time necessary to separate the solid matter.

⑦ Formulation
The recombinant human insulin is chemically modified. This produces a stable, aseptic compound that can be administered therapeutically via injection.

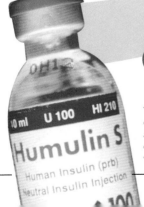

Recombinant antibiotics and vaccines
ARE ALSO PRODUCED BY GENETIC ENGINEERING.

DNA Markers

I n the past, individual plants in agriculture were chosen for reproduction according to visible characteristics or markers, such as the shape and color of fruit. Genetics demonstrated that these characteristics come from the expression of genes. The genes can also be accompanied by repeating groups of bases called DNA markers. These markers are useful primarily during the early phases of a plant's development to detect whether it has a certain trait. ●

 ## Preparation

Restriction enzymes are used to snip portions of DNA that have the microsatellite. After the microsatellite is isolated, it is multiplied into thousands of identical units using a process called polymerase chain reaction (PCR). This process is carried out with each of the samples obtained from different individuals to be compared. For example, comparing microsatellites from different tomato plants can show which individuals are heterozygotic or homozygotic or recessive or dominant for specific traits.

SAMPLE 1   SAMPLE 2   SAMPLE 3

Microsatellites

DNA has different types of molecular markers. Some of the most useful markers are called microsatellites. These markers are groups of up to 10 DNA bases that are repeated in short sequences. Microsatellites are very useful in evaluating plant and animal populations. For example, the length of a microsatellite shows whether given plants of the same species are homozygous or heterozygous for a certain trait. DNA markers are especially useful because they are not affected by the environment.

 ## Extraction

Molecular markers are extracted from DNA taken from a tissue sample. In the case of plants, even a tiny leaf may give enough DNA.

GA GA GA
GA GA GA
Microsatellite of a dominant homozygote.

GA GA GA
GA GA
Microsatellite of a heterozygotic individual

GA GA
GA GA
Microsatellite of a recessive homozygote

MOLECULAR MARKER
Repetitive sequence of a pair of bases (guanine [G] and adenine [A] in this example)

Based on Mendel

The Mendelian laws, essential to the development of the field of genetics, were discovered based on the markers of visible traits. These traits are very useful, except for a few disadvantages: they are based on an individual's phenotype (appearance), which is influenced by the environment. In addition, it is necessary to wait until a specimen is fully grown in order to find out whether it has a desired trait.

PARENT 1   PARENT 2

F 1

YELLOW
LARGE
The dominant allele is expressed.

RED
SMALL
This new trait may be of interest in a new crop.

RED
LARGE
The recessive allele is expressed.

3 Electrophoresis

Once the microsatellite samples are placed in the polyacrylamide gel, the gel is subjected to electrophoresis. This technique is widely used to separate molecules, in this case microsatellites, with a negative electrical charge by applying a current of electrons. When an electrical field is generated, electricity moves the microsatellites through the gel at different speeds. Their movement varies with the ratio of the electrical charge to the mass of each microsatellite. The lighter microsatellites travel farther than the longer ones.

POLYACRYLAMIDE GEL

MICROPIPETTE
This instrument is used to insert an exact amount of the DNA sample.

ELECTRIC CURRENT
The positive electrical charge attracts the negative charges in the gel.

DNA SAMPLE
Samples containing microsatellites and a substance that glows in UV light are scattered in a pocket of polyacrylamide gel.

4 Results

After electrophoresis is finished, the results can be examined by exposing the gel to ultraviolet light. The location of each microsatellite shows the relationship between the various samples analyzed. In this case, the samples show which alleles are present and which are not.

Sample 1 Sample 2 Sample 3

A MATCH
These microsatellites match. This shows that samples 2 and 3 share this allele.

NUMBER OF SAMPLES
More than 50 DNA samples can be placed for comparison in the same gel.

Kbp
250
225
200
175
150
125
100
75

Polymorphism

Variations in the sequence of a segment of DNA among the individuals of a population. For example, the variations in the color of tomatoes are a result of polymorphism.

Kbp
The unit of DNA molecular length

Genome in Sight!

One of the most far-reaching and extraordinary scientific achievements is the deciphering of the human genome. This is the complete set of hereditary information contained in the DNA of human chromosomes. In less than 20 years, with a combination of original genetic techniques and the power of computers, scientists glimpsed the location of all the genes, including those that determine eye color, hair type, blood type, and even a person's sex. ●

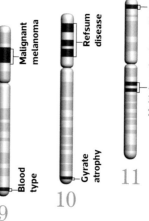

HUMAN
30,000 genes

Genetic dictionary

The 46 human chromosomes, together with mitochondrial DNA, contain all a human being's genetic information. Knowing the location and function of each gene or group of genes is useful for several reasons. It enables us to know if an illness stems from a defect in a gene or group of genes and even to correct the illness through gene therapy. We can also better understand any potential interaction among genes that are near each other in a chromosome and the effects of that interaction. Studying the human genome can even reveal the origin of our species among the primates.

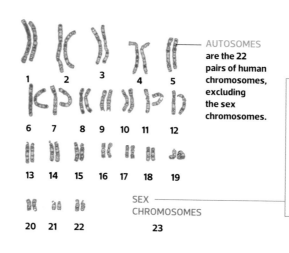

1 2 3 4 5

6 7 8 9 10 11 12

13 14 15 16 17 18 19

20 21 22

23

AUTOSOMES are the 22 pairs of human chromosomes, excluding the sex chromosomes.

SEX CHROMOSOMES

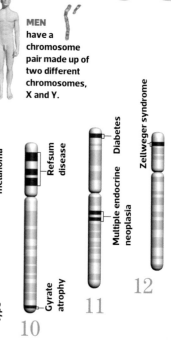

WOMEN have a pair of the same sex chromosome, called XX.

MEN have a chromosome pair made up of two different chromosomes, X and Y.

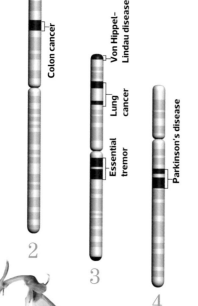

Gaucher's disease

Colon cancer

Alzheimer's disease

1

2

Von Hippel–Lindau disease

Lung cancer

Essential tremor

3

Parkinson's disease

4

Steroid 5-alpha-reductase

Asthma

Dystrophic dysplasia

5

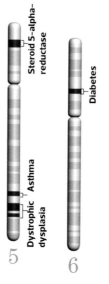

Diabetes

6

Diabetes

Language development

Obesity

7

Werner's syndrome

Burkitt lymphoma

8

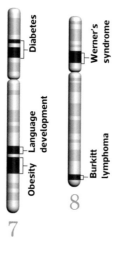

Malignant melanoma

Blood type

9

Refsum disease

Gyrate atrophy

10

Multiple endocrine neoplasia

Diabetes

11

Zellweger syndrome

12

Gregor Mendel is rediscovered by Tschermak, De Vries, and Correns.

Drosophila melanogaster, **the fruit fly,** is the subject of experiments by T.H. Morgan based on chromosomal theory.

James Watson and Francis Crick propose a structural model of DNA.

Discovery that the human species has **46 chromosomes**

The first description of **a restriction enzyme**

John Gurdon first used somatic nuclei to create **clones** of an amphibian larva.

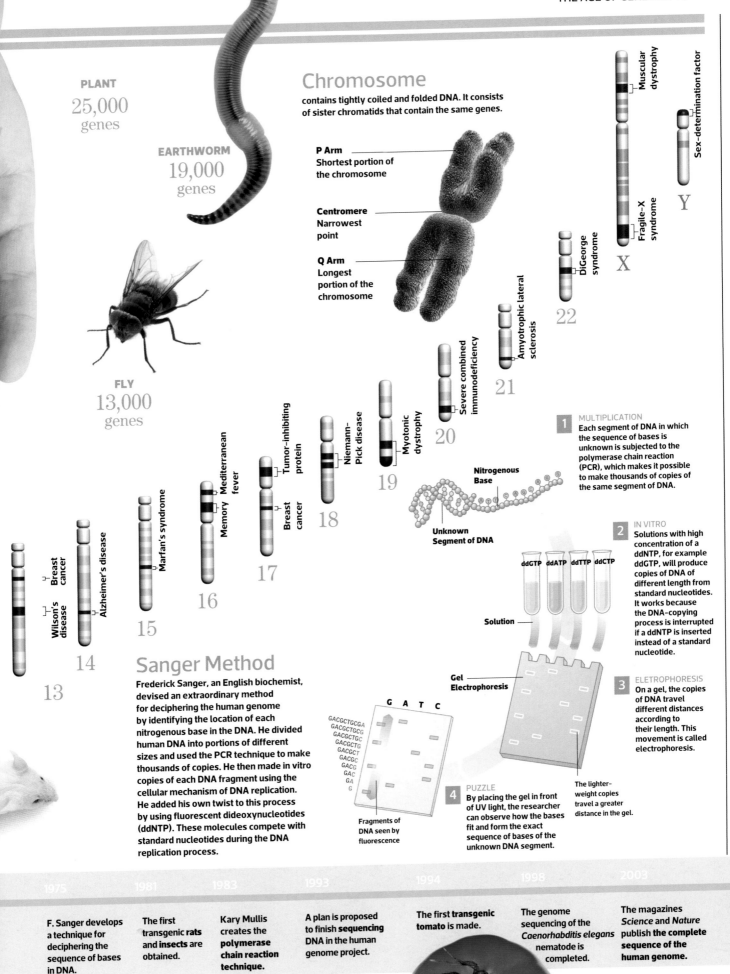

Chromosome

contains tightly coiled and folded DNA. It consists of sister chromatids that contain the same genes.

P Arm
Shortest portion of the chromosome

Centromere
Narrowest point

Q Arm
Longest portion of the chromosome

PLANT
25,000 genes

EARTHWORM
19,000 genes

FLY
13,000 genes

Muscular dystrophy

Sex-determination factor

Fragile-X syndrome

X

Y

DiGeorge syndrome

22

Amyotrophic lateral sclerosis

21

Severe combined immunodeficiency

20

Myotonic dystrophy

19

Niemann-Pick disease

18

Tumor-inhibiting protein

Breast cancer

17

Mediterranean fever

Memory

16

Marfan's syndrome

15

Breast cancer

Alzheimer's disease

Wilson's disease

14

13

Nitrogenous Base

Unknown Segment of DNA

1 MULTIPLICATION
Each segment of DNA in which the sequence of bases is unknown is subjected to the polymerase chain reaction (PCR), which makes it possible to make thousands of copies of the same segment of DNA.

2 IN VITRO
Solutions with high concentration of a ddNTP, for example ddGTP, will produce copies of DNA of different length from standard nucleotides. It works because the DNA-copying process is interrupted if a ddNTP is inserted instead of a standard nucleotide.

ddGTP ddATP ddTTP ddCTP

Solution

3 ELETROPHORESIS
On a gel, the copies of DNA travel different distances according to their length. This movement is called electrophoresis.

Gel Electrophoresis

Sanger Method

Frederick Sanger, an English biochemist, devised an extraordinary method for deciphering the human genome by identifying the location of each nitrogenous base in the DNA. He divided human DNA into portions of different sizes and used the PCR technique to make thousands of copies. He then made in vitro copies of each DNA fragment using the cellular mechanism of DNA replication. He added his own twist to this process by using fluorescent dideoxynucleotides (ddNTP). These molecules compete with standard nucleotides during the DNA replication process.

G A T C

GACGCTGCGA
GACGCTGCG
GACGCTGC
GACGCTG
GACGCT
GACGC
GACG
GAC
GA
G

Fragments of DNA seen by fluorescence

4 PUZZLE
By placing the gel in front of UV light, the researcher can observe how the bases fit and form the exact sequence of bases of the unknown DNA segment.

The lighter-weight copies travel a greater distance in the gel.

1975 F. Sanger develops a technique for deciphering the sequence of bases in DNA.

1981 The first transgenic **rats** and **insects** are obtained.

1983 **Kary Mullis** creates the **polymerase chain reaction** technique.

1993 A plan is proposed to finish **sequencing** DNA in the human genome project.

1994 The first **transgenic tomato** is made.

1998 The genome sequencing of the *Caenorhabditis elegans* nematode is completed.

2003 The magazines *Science* and *Nature* publish **the complete sequence of the human genome.**

Stem Cells

The reasoning is simple: if an organism with more than 200 different types of cells is formed from a group of embryonic cells without specialization, then manipulating the division of these original cells (called stem cells) should make it possible to generate all the human tissues and even produce autotransplants with minimal risk. Although such work is in progress, the results are far from being a medical reality. Scientists all over the world are studying its application. ●

EMBRYONIC CELLS
This photograph shows the eye of a needle with an embryo formed only by stem cells before cellular differentiation begins.

Cellular Division

All the cells of higher organisms divide and multiply through mitosis, with the exception of the reproductive gametes. Mitosis is the process through which a cell divides to form two identical cells. For this to happen, the first cell copies its genetic material inside the nucleus, and later it slowly partitions until it fully divides, producing two cells with the same genetic material. An adult cell divides on average 20 times before dying; a stem cell does it indefinitely.

CYTOPLASM

STEM CELLS

NUCLEUS
contains the DNA. First it duplicates the DNA, and then it divides.

② Multiplication

Once isolated, stem cells are cultivated in vitro under special conditions. It is common to resort to a substrate of irradiated cells, which serve as support without competing for space. Later, every seven days, they need to be separated to keep them from dying and to be able to reproduce them.

16 cells

IS THE LIMIT FOR CULTIVATION. THIS LIMITATION GUARANTEES THE ABSENCE OF A HUMAN EMBRYO. THE EXACT NUMBER IS DEBATED.

① Obtaining

Because the stem cells are the first that form after fertilization occurs, they are abundant in the placenta and especially in the umbilical cord. Geneticists obtain them from the cord once the baby has been born, and it is possible to freeze the cord to harvest the stem cells later.

UMBILICAL CORD
There are many stem cells because they are not differentiated.

MITOSIS
The cells multiply according to their genetic program.

STEM CELL

③ Differentiation

The stem cells are pluripotent, which is to say that they have the power to create any of the more than 200 different cells of the body. This process happens as the embryo grows. If the optimal conditions could be created in vitro, it would be possible to form in a laboratory all the cells of the body using the genetic program of the cells. In practice, this technique is possible only with a few types of cells, in particular blood cells.

ACTIVATORS
Chemical and hormonal activators guide the specialization.

NEURONS
have yet to be grown in the laboratory.

THERE ARE MORE THAN

200

TYPES OF CELLS IN THE HUMAN BODY

WHITE BLOOD CELL
Some tests have managed to produce them.

RED BLOOD CELL
Generating them in vitro has been achieved.

STEM CELLS
divide indefinitely without losing their properties.

FIRST USE
In 1998 stem cells were isolated and cultivated for the first time in the United States. Since then, numerous laboratories in the world have cultivated them. Because of ethical questions that surround work with embryonic cells, each line is monitored through official organizations.

1998
27 lines

2000

2003

2006 225 lines

④ Implantation

Doctors and geneticists hope to be able to provide new pluripotent cells to damaged tissue and provoke its regeneration. To date, they have been able to introduce umbilical-cord hematopoietic stem cells into patients with dysfunctional formation of red blood cells. This is equivalent to a bone marrow transplant without surgical intervention.

BLOOD
Reproduced in vitro, the stem cells are then injected.

HEART
Stem cells are being used to repair the heart after an infarction.

Cow Cloning

The term "cloning" itself provokes controversy. Strictly speaking, to clone is to obtain an identical organism from another through technology. The most commonly used technique is called somatic-cell nuclear transfer. It was used to create Dolly the sheep as well as other cloned animals, including these Jersey cows. The technique consists of replacing the nucleus of an ovule with the nucleus of a cell from a donor specimen. When the ovule then undergoes division, it gives rise to an organism identical to the donor. With all such processes, there exist slight differences between the donor and the clone. In only one case is the clone perfect, and it comes naturally: monozygous (identical) twins. ●

① Obtaining the Nucleus

A specialized cell of an adult animal, whose DNA is complete, is isolated, and it is cultivated in vitro to multiply it. Various ovules of a donor cow are also isolated. The nucleus is then removed from both groups of cells—only those of adult cells.

② Nucleus Transfer

Consists of replacing the nucleus of the ovule with that obtained from the adult cell. In this form, the chromosomes carried by the new nucleus complete the ovule in the same way as if the ovule had been fertilized by a spermatozoon. Once fused, the cell will begin its program of division as if it were a zygote (fertilized ovule).

NUCLEUS OF THE CELL TO CLONE
The nucleus is transferred to the ovule.

NUCLEUS EXTRACTION
A fibroblast is extracted from the ear of an exemplary adult.

Nucleus with Complete DNA (60 chromosomes)

Ovule Without Nucleus

OVULE EXTRACTION
An ovule is obtained from the ovary of another exemplary specimen, and the nucleus is removed.

OVULE WITHOUT NUCLEUS
Only the cytoplasm, with organelles like mitochondria, remains.

PIPETTE
supports the ovule and prevents it from shifting in the operation.

Cost

The technology is still not efficient. For this Jersey, 934 ovules were transferred, of which 166 fused, and only one developed successfully.

DIVERSE USES

Cloning can be applied for obtaining new organisms and tissues and for reproducing segments of DNA.

PIPETTE
It is used to introduce the nucleus into the ovule.

16 cells

④ Cultivation

The new cell is cultivated in vitro, where it multiplies until forming a blastocyst (cellular group whose cells are not yet differentiated by function and is a precursor to an embryo). The developing blastocyst is maintained in a medium that contains hormones and 5 percent oxygen to simulate the conditions of a cow's uterus. After a week, the developing mass has become large enough that it can be implanted into the actual uterus of a cow.

8 cells

2 cells

⑤ Insemination

The blastocyst is implanted in the uterus of a donor cow on the sixth day after the cow has stopped being in heat so that the development of the blastocyst continues in a natural way. If everything goes as planned, the blastocyst adheres to the uterine wall.

③ Fusion

By means of light electric discharges, fusion of the donated nucleus with the cytoplasm of the ovule is initiated. Three hours later, calcium is added to the cell to simulate fertilization. An interchange begins between the nucleus and the cytoplasm, and the cell starts to divide.

RECTUM

OVIDUCT

OVARY

INFUNDIBULUM

UTERUS

BLASTOCYST

CERVIX

VAGINA   PIPETTE

BLADDER

⑥ Development of the Fetus

Once the blastocyst is implanted, its growth begins. The normal period of gestation for a cow is from 280 to 290 days. Because all the genetic information required was provided by a donor-cell nucleus, the calf that is born is an exact copy of the donor animal. It differs only in the mitochondrial DNA, which was provided by the receptor ovule.

Biochip Applications

D evices that use a small, flat substrate (chip) that contains biological (bio) material are commonly called biochips. Biochips are used for obtaining genetic information. A biochip is a type of miniaturized equipment that integrates tens of thousands of probes made up of genetic material having a known sequence. When the probes are placed in contact with a biological sample (such as from a patient or experiment), only the nucleotide chains complementary to those of the chip hybridize. This action produces a characteristic pattern light, which is read with a scanner and interpreted by a computer. ●

2 Samples

A microinjector fills each one of the pores in the biochip with samples of the different sequences of genes from the organism.

SMALL SIZE
Biochips are the size of a stamp and are contained in a glass structure.

0.2 inch
(4.5 mm)

0.3 inch
(6.4 mm)

BioChip

MASK
Template with microarray of cells

PHOTODEGRADABLE FILM
functions as an intermediary layer.

GLASS SUBSTRATE
is chemically treated with certain reactive groups to permit the implantation of the oligonucleotides.

1 Procedure

This biochip has a template, or pattern—called a genetic microarray—that makes it possible to compare the DNA of one tissue sample from a person with the genes that cause a disease. In the case of a particular type of cancer, for example, researchers want to know the genes that are involved in the disease.

NORMAL
The cDNA (complimentary DNA) of normal cells is colored with a green fluorescent marking.

Cells of Normal Tissue

Cells of Cancerous Tissue

CANCER
The cDNA of cancerous cells is colored with a red fluorescent marking.

MIX
The tubes of green and red markings are combined in the same tube.

Mv4000i

COMPUTER
The pattern is input into a special computer where the microinjectors will take care of filling the 96 orifices, or spots, on the biochip.

3 Microinjection

Through microinjection, each spot is filled with cDNA marker of both fluorescent substances (coming from cancerous and normal tissues combined).

COLOR FILTER

4 How It Works

Once the injection of the marking mix is finished, it is necessary to detect which stuck to what spot. For this, the array is placed in a scanner with a green and a red laser, which excite the fluorescent targets. The microscope and the camera work in conjunction to create an image, and this information is stored in a computer.

LIGHT RAYS

Spots filled with cDNA marked with both fluorescent substances

GREEN
The gene found in this spot expresses normal conditions.

RED
The gene found in this spot expresses cancerous conditions.

YELLOW
The gene found in this spot expresses normal conditions together with those of cancer.

5 Results

All the points of the marked biochip have small sequences of DNA that are compared with a sequence of the samples. The fluorescent signals, detected by means of a computer, indicate which of the DNA sequences on the chip have complementary sequences in the sample. A special program is used to calculate the proportion of red to green fluorescent signals in the image.

Gene Therapy

O ne of the latest breakthroughs in medicine, gene therapy is used to introduce genetic material to correct deficiencies of one or more defective genes that are the cause of an illness. Several different techniques have been developed for use with human patients, almost all of which are at the research stage. The problem with illnesses with a genetic origin is that therapy must modify the cells of the affected organ. To reach all these cells, or a significant number of them, demands elaborate protocols or, as is the case for viruses, the use of nature's biological weapons to cause other illnesses. ●

HERPESVIRUS
The herpesvirus is an icosahedral virus and holds a DNA sequence that needs to be modified so that it will not cause an illness. It is widely used in gene therapy.

Treatable Illnesses

Illnesses with a genetic origin are difficult to treat, since the organism has poorly coded genes and the fault is therefore present in all its cells. Cystic fibrosis and Duchenne muscular dystrophy are examples of monogenetic illnesses that can potentially be treated with these therapies.

Gene therapy has also been attempted on cancer and HIV infection, among other pathologies. A definitive cure may be found for many genetic illnesses, but the techniques for gene therapy are still in the development stage.

3 Replacement

The modified adenovirus is inoculated in a cell culture to generate the viral infection. It then enters the cells and multiplies in the cytoplasm, copying its DNA, including the modification carried in the cassette, in the nucleus of the infected cell, where it transcribes the new information.

ADENOVIRUS
Its genetic makeup is modified so it can carry the sequence that will be introduced.

NUCLEAR PORE

DNA
holds the sequence that repairs the targeted gene.

MODIFIED DNA

CELL NUCLEUS

1 Identification

The DNA sequence that corresponds to the gene that causes the deficiency requiring treatment is identified. Then the correct sequence is isolated and multiplied to guarantee a quantity that can modify the organism. Because a monogenetic illness generally affects the function of one organ, the cell volume that is targeted for modification is large. Then a technique is chosen to transfect the cells.

2 Vehicle

An adenovirus is an icosahedral virus that contains double-stranded DNA and lacks an outer envelope. It is primarily the cause of a number of mild respiratory illnesses. If the virus can be modified to be nonpathogenic, it has the potential for use in transporting a modified sequence of DNA in a region called a cassette. Even though its capacity is limited, its effectiveness rate is very high.

AFFECTED CELL

DNA TRANSCRIPTION

1 Damaged gene to be modified

2 Added healthy gene

Synthesis

The infected culture cells, which have the
new genetic information, can now synthesize
the compound that caused the dysfunction.
Generally these are proteins that cannot
be synthesized because the gene for their
elaboration is disassociated or damaged.
The process begins once the cells divide and
transcribe the gene in question. The protein
that was not synthesized before is now
transcribed and produced.

NEW
HEALTHY
CELL

MODIFIED
DNA

Relationship

It is critical that the hypothetical number of cells to
be modified and the number of viruses needed for
the therapy to work are in the correct relationship.

PROTEIN
The absence of a protein
that results from a
genetic error and the
failure to synthesize the
protein can have serious
consequences.

NEW
HEALTHY
CELL

MODIFIED
DNA

Kilobase

The unit in which DNA and RNA are
measured; the capacity of a virus's
cassette, which on average is
approximately five kilobases.

NONVIRAL GENE THERAPIES

Many are based on physical means such as electrical
techniques. They have the advantage of producing
material in vitro, which allows for a large transfer
capacity not limited by the number of bases that can
be transfected by a virus. The problem is that these
methods are not efficient for reaching target cells in the
organism. The most important therapies of this type
are microinjection, calcium phosphate precipitation, and
electroporation (the use of an electric field to increase
the permeability of the cell membrane).

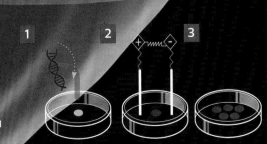

DNA Footprints

Since Sir Alec Jeffreys developed the concept of the DNA profile for the identification of people, this type of forensic technique has taken on significant importance. A practically unmistakable genetic footprint can be established that allows for the correlation of evidence found at the scene of a crime (hair, semen, blood samples) with a suspect. In addition, the use of this technique is a key element to determine the genetic link in kin relationships.●

SWAB
For saliva samples. Then it is immersed in a solvent solution and the DNA extracted.

1 Sample Collection

Any body fluid, such as urine, blood, semen, sweat, and saliva, or fragments, such as tissues, cells, or hairs, can be analyzed to obtain a person's DNA. There is generally always something left at the scene that can be used as a sample.

Only a very small amount of evidence is needed for sampling. For example, just a small fraction of a drop of blood or sperm is sufficient.

Each sample is placed in separate plastic bags, sealed, and certified to avoid adulterations.

FACTORS THAT ALTER DNA

Moisture or water will denaturalize a sample faster.

Heat is one of the most destructive factors.

2 DNA Separation

HAIR FOLLICLE
A follicle has DNA that is easy to obtain.

TWEEZERS
must be properly sterilized.

1 HAIR DIGESTION
The hair is divided into sections. These are then put into a tube, and solvents are applied.

MICROPIPETTE
Only the substance floating on the surface is extracted. This is where the DNA is.

LABELING
is absolutely necessary so that the samples are not mixed up.

2 CENTRIFUGING
The suspended DNA must be centrifuged to separate it from the rest of the cell material.

3 PRECIPITATION
A 95 percent solution of ethanol is added; the sample is shaken and then centrifuged at a higher speed than before.

Surface-floating substance and pellet

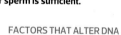

③ DNA Magnification

The polymerase chain reaction (PCR) is carried out by a machine that, using heat, synthetic short nucleotide sequences, and enzymes, copies each fragment of DNA as many times as needed. This amplification makes it possible to conduct a large number of tests while conserving the DNA. Later the DNA fragments are separated by means of capillary electrophoresis.

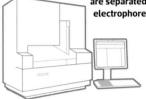

Visualization of the DNA as curves on the monitor

DNA-EVIDENCE GRAPH

The numbers represent a position in the DNA sequence.

100   105   110

C T C T A C G G T G T C G G G C C T

CYTOSINE   **GUANINE**

THIAMINE   **ADENINE**

④ Impression and Comparison

The machine presents the results as curves, where each base has a specific location according to the height of the curve in the graph sequence. It then compares the sample obtained at the crime scene with those obtained from the crime suspects. If one of them was at the scene of the crime, the curves coincide exactly in at least 13 known positions.

DNA GRAPH FOR SUSPECT A

○ **COINCIDENCE OF GENETIC PATTERNS**

13 locations

is the minimum number of coinciding points that need to be found for a suspect to be accused of a crime in the United States.

DNA GRAPH FOR SUSPECT B

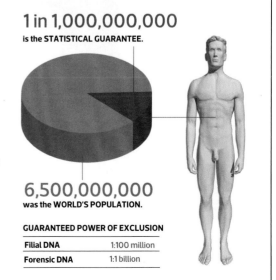

DISPOSABLE MATERIAL
All the material that is used must be disposable to avoid contaminating the DNA.

4 SURFACE-FLOATING SUBSTANCE
A 70 percent solution of ethanol is added, and the mixture is rinsed with water. The DNA is free of impurities and ready for analysis.

DNA and pellet of leftover materials

Power of Exclusion (PE)

Overall, for a DNA test to be considered as valid criminal evidence, at least in theory, it should be able to guarantee a PE with a certainty above 99.9999999 percent. The PE is measured as a percentage but is expressed as the number of people who are excluded as possible bearers of the DNA at the crime scene. Thus, a sample is taken at random from one person, as a type of witness, and it is then compared with the DNA from the evidence and that of the suspect. The detail of the analysis must be so precise that it can, at least theoretically, be able to discriminate one person among one billion people. In practice, the test is valid if it statistically discriminates one person in one billion. All this is done to guarantee the results of the test and so that it can have validity in court. In practice, the suspects are not chosen randomly but fulfill other evidence patterns, among which DNA is used to confirm these patterns.

1 in 1,000,000,000
is the STATISTICAL GUARANTEE.

6,500,000,000
was the WORLD'S POPULATION.

GUARANTEED POWER OF EXCLUSION

Filial DNA	1:100 million
Forensic DNA	1:1 billion

Modified Foods

G enetically modified foods have always existed. An example is wine, modified through the fermentation of grapes. However, modern biotechnology based on DNA decoding has made these processes predictable and controllable. The process improves specific characteristics of the plant, makes it more resistant to pests, and improves its nutritional quality. The objective is a greater production of food with better agronomic and nutritional characteristics. ●

Bacteria

Recombinant plasmids

More benefits

The development of transgenic plants has allowed the production of food with more vitamins, minerals, and proteins, or with less fat. The development of genetic technology has also been able to delay the maturation of fruits and vegetables and, in other cases, make them more resistant to specific pests, thus reducing the need for applying insecticides to crops. The genetic modification of some crops also produces smaller and stronger plants, while simultaneously increasing their yield, because they invest more energy into producing their edible parts.

CONJUGATIVE PLASMIDS
The plasmids are mixed with DNA bits to form conjugative plasmids.

ELECTRICAL PULSES
Bacteria are added, and quick electrical pulses are applied that cause the plasmids with the transgene to enter the bacteria.

Test tube

The marine strawberry

Research has been conducted in modifying strawberries with a gene from the plaice to make the fruit more resistant to frost. This is a simple process from which the crop yields can be improved by a high percentage.

RESTRICTION ENZYME
The enzyme is added to the cloned DNA in a test tube to segment or divide it into pieces the size of the gene. The bacterial plasmids that were extracted using the same enzyme are added in another test tube.

1 The gene that keeps the plaice from freezing is copied and spliced into a plasmid taken from a bacterium.

Bacteria DNA

2 The plasmid from the bacterium that holds the plaice gene is then inserted onto a second bacterium.

Antifreezing gene

❶ Cloning the Desired Gene

All the DNA is extracted from the *Bacillus thuringiensis* bacteria in order to locate and copy the gene responsible for this characteristic.

Second bacterium

3 A strawberry cell culture is infected with the antifreezing gene. This is then integrated into the strawberry DNA, and plant transgenesis takes place.

bacterium *Bacillus thuringiensis*

DNA

Desired Gene

Strawberry cell

Antifreezing gene

4 The new transgenic strawberry can reproduce as many times as it wants.

Bt Corn

has been genetically modified to make it resistant to the western corn rootworm, a pest that feeds on the root of the plant. Bt corn produces the Bt toxin, a toxin naturally produced by a soil bacterium. The pest is killed either when the larvae attempt to feed on the root or the adults attempt to feed on the foliage of the Bt corn.

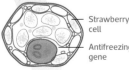

Endogenous Bacterial Plasmid

Plasmid with Insect Toxin Transgene

Petri Dish

DESIRED GENE
Bacteria multiply to obtain a copy of each one of the thousands of genes from the organism. The desired gene is located and hundreds of copies are made.

TRANSGENIC BACTERIA
Recombinant plasmids enter the bacteria that will express the genes.

The labels
Transgenic foods have their own label. This is a legal requirement in most countries. When the time comes to shop for fruits, vegetables, or cereals at the supermarket, we must look closely at the labels. In the case of corn or rice, only 9 percent should be transgenic. This should be clearly explained in the list of ingredients.

Genfood

❷ Modified Gene Design
The gene is composed of a codified sequence (wanted gene) and of regulatory sequences, which can be altered for the gene to be expressed in a desired form. The selected gene confers an advantage, for instance, resistance to an herbicide.

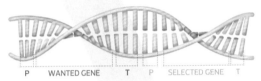

P   WANTED GENE   T   P   SELECTED GENE   T

❸ Transformation
The modified gene is inserted into the nucleus of the corn cell so that it can be incorporated into some of the chromosomes. For this effect, the gene pistol, or gene cannon, is used.

Hundreds of gold particles are covered or plated with thousands of copies of the new gene.

Gold Particle

The gold particles are shot toward the cell sample.

Corn Cell Culture

If the particle enters the nucleus, the genes are dissolved and can be incorporated into the chromosomes' DNA.

Chromosome

Nucleus

❹ Culture
The transgenic corn cells are distributed in crop media that contain the necessary nutrients. Those that proliferate form a whole plant from transformed cells. The adult transgenic plants are transplanted to the agricultural fields. This transgenic corn and its descendants will be resistant to the western corn rootworm.

Golden rice
Golden rice is the first organism that was modified genetically for the purpose of providing an increased level of vitamin A for populations with a deficiency in the vitamin. The embryo of golden rice stores beta carotene and other carotenes, which are the precursors of vitamin A.

1 The genes used are those that encode for the enzymes phytoene synthase and lycopene synthase in the plant *Narcissus pseudonarcissus* and the enzyme carotene desaturase from *Erwinia uredovona* bacteria.

Narcissus pseudonarcissus

Erwinia uredovona

2 The DNA strands from these genes are inserted into plasmids, which are later introduced into *Agrobacterium tumefaciens* bacteria.

Plasmids

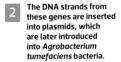

3 Agrobacteria are inoculated into immature rice crop embryos.

Agrobacteria

4 Transgenic plants are obtained from these crop embryos, which generate transgenic rice grains with extra vitamin A in its endosperm.

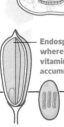

Endosperm where vitamin A accumulates

Pharmaceutical Farms

A transgenic animal is one in which foreign genes have been introduced through genetic engineering, integrated into the animal's genome, and transmitted from generation to generation. The first achievements in this field were made with cell cultures, and the first "whole" animal that was obtained with an exogenous gene was a rat. Other mammals, such as rabbits, pigs, cows, sheep, goats, and monkeys, are being genetically manipulated for medical or animal–production purposes.

Pigs to cure hemophilia

Scientists at the Pharmaceutical Engineering Institute of Virginia Tech and colleagues added the gene for the factor VIII protein of human coagulation to a few transgenic pigs. This protein is of vital therapeutic importance as a coagulant agent for type A hemophiliacs.

Human gene for factor VIII

Gene for factor VIII

1 FACTOR VIII is identified and the gene copied. A procedure is then worked out to cause this gene to be expressed only in the mammary gland of the pigs so that the factor is produced in their milk.

Low Cost

The proteins of factor VIII and factor IX that are injected into patients with hemophilia come from human blood plasma and are very costly. In contrast, in the future, an injection of such proteins purified from the milk of transgenic livestock could cost only a dollar per injection.

2 ANIMAL TRANSGENESIS is accomplished with the microinjection of the human gene of factor VIII directly into fertilized ovules, so that the sequence integrates into its genome.

3 IMPLANT The ovule is implanted in the uterus of an adoptive mother, which has been hormonally prepared.

4 BIRTH Once the female transgenic pigs are born, it is necessary to verify that they have at least one copy of the transgene.

5 MILK WITH FACTOR VIII When adulthood is reached, the female pig produces milk with factor VIII, which can help those sick with hemophilia.

TRANSGENIC PIGS
Investigators at the Pharmaceutical Engineering Institute of Virginia Tech hold three of the specimens.

Hypoallergenic Cats

Cat lovers who have not been able to fulfill their dreams of having a cat as a pet because of their allergies are given a hint of a hopeful smile. A company is selling genetically engineered cats that it claims produce a very low level of a saliva protein, which is the cause of allergic reactions in humans.

Spiders with threads of steel

Recombinant spider silk, called BioSteel, has been produced from the milk of goats implanted with the gene of the spider *Nephila clavipes*, commonly known as the golden thread spider. Similar to natural spider silk, the product was reported to be five times stronger but lighter than steel, silky in texture, and biodegradable.

6

FACTOR VIII
is extracted from the milk. The protein is purified and the desired pharmacological product obtained.

Fluorescent rats

The Research Institute for Microbial Diseases at Osaka University, Japan, obtained the GFP (green fluorescent protein) gene of the jellyfish *Aequorea victoria*. The gene was introduced in the fertilized ovules of the female rat, which gestates an animal that will have green fluorescent skin under UV light. One application was to mark cancer cells and see how they travel around the body.

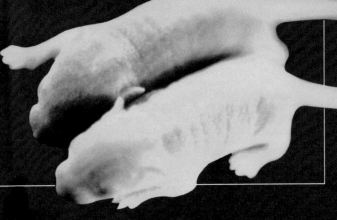

The Genetic Ancestor

Ever since Darwin published his theory about the evolution of species, humans have sought to understand their origin in light of a diversity of ideas and theories. With the success of efforts to map the human genome, old evidence is gaining new strength. Many scientific teams used some 100,000 samples of DNA from all over the world to trace the process of human expansion back to a common ancestor—the "Mitochondrial Eve" that lived in sub-Saharan Africa some 150,000 years ago. She was not the only human female of her time, but she was the one that all present-day women recognize as a common genetic ancestor. The key to the trail is in DNA mutations.

Genetic material

Each time an organism is conceived, its genetic material is a fusion of equal parts received from its parents. Recovering this material throughout history is impossible because of the large number of combinations, so scientists use mitochondrial DNA from the cells as well as DNA from the chromosomes. Thus, following a single path for each sex, the possible combinations are reduced to a set of hereditary lines that are traceable over time. This method is possible when a cell's DNA, along with the various locations of the genes and recombinant areas, is known.

Ovule
This cell is a haploid cell that at the moment of fertilization provides the cellular organelles as well as half of the chromosomes. Among the organelles, the mitochondria are the most important for genetic studies.

Spermatozoon
When a spermatozoon fertilizes an ovule, its tail breaks off, along with all cellular material except its nucleus, which contains half of the necessary genetic information for a new individual.

Mitochondria
are the organelles that provide energy to the cell through respiration. They contain a portion of DNA.

Haplotype

is a set of closely linked alleles on a chromosome.

Recombinant Region

Recombinant Region

Nonrecombinant Region

Recombinant Region

The Y chromosome

A baby's sex is determined by the sperm cell that succeeds in fertilizing the ovule. Specifically the male gender is determined by the Y chromosome, which is passed on from father to son. To follow a line of ascendant mutations in the recombinant part, the markers of each mutation must be read from the ends to the center to find a common male ancestor. He is called the chromosomal Adam, and he is estimated to have lived 60,000 to 90,000 years ago in Africa.

Mitochondrial DNA

Mitochondria contain circular DNA. This DNA has two hypervariable regions called HVR 1 and HVR 2, where mutations can happen. Over time, the mutations leave marks that can be traced according to their location from the ends to the center. Because mitochondria are inherited from the mother, the mutations can be traced back to a female genetic ancestor. This "Mitochondrial Eve" lived in sub-Saharan Africa about 150,000 to 200,000 years ago. She was not alone at the time, nor was she the only one of her species. However, she was the only one of her community whose genetic inheritance survives.

Genetic Diversity and Phylogenetics

Geneticists have determined statistically that every three generations there is a mutation that will be preserved in the DNA of the descendants. They used this statistic and demographic studies to calculate the age of the "Mitochondrial Eve" and the "Nuclear Adam." If the path of mutations is followed from the present to the past, the line of ascent would lead to these genetic ancestors. However, in reverse, many mutations represent dead ends. That is, they left no descendants for a wide range of reasons. These links are part of the study called phylogenetics and make up well-defined haplogroups. Each haplogroup represents the genetic diversity of a species.

Great-grandparents
First Generation

Grandparents
Second Generation

Parents
Third Generation
According to scientific calculations, this is when genetic mutations may occur.

Children
Fourth Generation

Other chromosomes

Y chromosome
Mitochondrial DNA

Paternal Line   Maternal Line

Genetic drift

Each time a mutation occurs, it continues as a mark on future generations. Genetic drift explains how this mutation spreads and how the effectiveness of its spread is related to the number of individuals in a group, the time they live in a certain region, and the environment. If the group is small, its chances of success are increased because genetic drift is more effective in changing the genetic pattern. Also, the longer the group remains in one place, the more mutations it will have.

Africa is where the greatest number of mutations is found. This leads to the supposition that humans have lived there the longest.

Haplogroup

is a human group with the same genetic descent, recognized by characteristic mutations.

L0 and L1, the most ancient
These haplogroups have the greatest number of mutations in their DNA and are the oldest human groups. They are the San and Khoekhoe peoples in Africa.

50,000-70,000 years ago
They migrate to other continents via the Red Sea.

Homo sapiens is found only in Africa.

30,000-40,000 years ago
They spread to the rest of the world.

The common relative

In genetic terms, DNA enables us to conceive of a primordial Adam and Eve, our genetic ancestors. However, the common ancestor of all humans alive today is quite a different matter. Several scientific hypotheses estimate that an ancestor to whom we are all related lived between 1,000 and 10,000 years ago.

Glossary

Acid

Type of chemical compound. DNA, vinegar, and lemon juice are weak acids.

Adaptation

A particular characteristic of an organism's structure, physiology, or behavior that enables it to live in its environment.

Allele

One of several alternatives of a gene. For example, the gene for eye color can have brown and blue alleles.

Amino Acid

One of the 20 chemical compounds that living beings use to form proteins.

Anthropologist

Scientist who studies human beings from the viewpoint of their social and biological relationships.

Archaeologist

Scientist who studies human history based on the objects humans have left behind, such as buildings, ceramics, and weapons.

Artificial Fertilization

Technique for fertilizing ovules. It is usually done in vitro, after which the fertilized ovule is implanted.

Artificial Selection

As opposed to natural selection, human intervention in the process of speciation; breeding animals or plants to improve their traits is an example.

Bacteria

One-celled organisms that are prokaryotic (they lack a nucleus bound by a membrane). Some cause illnesses, others are harmless, and still others are beneficial.

Bacteriophage

Virus that only infects bacteria; used as a vector in genetic engineering.

Bioballistics

Recombinant genetic technique that consists of shooting small metal projectiles covered with DNA into a cell to penetrate the nucleus and recombine the genes in the desired manner.

Biologist

Scientist who studies living beings.

Bioprospecting

The taking of tissue samples from living beings to find genes that can be patented to obtain economic benefits.

Cell

Smallest independent unit that forms part of a living being.

Cell Nucleus

The central part of a cell, it contains the chromosomes and regulates the cell's activity. In some cells it is well differentiated. Other cells, such as some bacteria and red blood cells, have no nucleus.

Cellular Membrane

Flexible covering of all living cells that contains the cytoplasm. It is semipermeable and regulates the interchange of water and gases with the outside.

Chimera

In Greek mythology, a monster with the head of a lion, the body of a goat, and the tail of a serpent. In genetics, the hypothetical creation of one being from the parts of others.

Chromosomal Crossover

A step during meiosis that corresponds to the interchange of genes between diploid chromosomes and causes the recombination of genes.

Chromosome

Sequence of DNA coiled inside the nucleus of a cell. One cell usually has more than one chromosome, and together they make up the genetic inheritance of an individual.

Clone

A living being that is identical to another. It also refers to parts, such as organs or fragments of DNA, that are identical.

Cloning

Action of producing a clone.

Coevolution

When more than one species evolve together, and the changes in one cause the others to undergo modifications in mutual adaptation.

Cytoplasm

Watery or gelatinous substance that contains organelles and makes up most of the interior of the cell, except for the nucleus.

Cytosine

One of the four bases that make up the DNA molecule.

Descendant

Family member belonging to later generations, such as a child, grandchild, or great-grandchild.

Designer Baby

Human baby selected as an embryo based on a set of genetic traits chosen before its birth.

Diabetes

Disease that prevents the body from synthesizing the necessary amount of insulin, a protein essential for the body's proper functioning.

Diploid

Cell with two complete sets of chromosomes. It is represented by the symbol 2n.

DNA

Deoxyribonucleic acid; molecule in the shape of a double helix with codified genetic information.

DNA Footprint

The identification of a person by DNA; used in forensics.

DNA Sequencing

Obtaining the structure of bases that make up DNA. The long DNA chain is often divided into smaller fractions for study.

Dominant Gene

Gene that, when present in a pair of alleles, is always manifested.

Double Helix

Shape of two spirals in geometric space. The DNA chain has this shape.

Dyslexia

Disorder, sometimes genetically based, that causes difficulties with reading, writing, and speech.

Embryo

Product of an ovule fertilized by a sperm cell. It can develop into an adult organism.

Endoplasmic Reticulum

Group of narrow channels that transport various types of substances and molecules from one point to another inside a cell.

Enzyme

Protein that helps regulate the chemical processes in a cell.

Escherichia coli

Abundant bacteria often used in genetic experiments.

Eugenics

Science that seeks to improve humankind by selecting and controlling human genes. Its objectives are highly controversial.

Evolution

Gradual change in a species or organism; not necessarily an improvement. It was theorized by Darwin in his famous book *On the Origin of Species*.

Extinction

The disappearance of all specimens of one or more species.

Fertilization

Fusion of a male gamete with a female gamete, forming a zygote, which can develop into a new individual.

Filler DNA

Long, repeated sequences of DNA that do not provide genetic information. Also called junk DNA.

Forensics

Scientific discipline of the study of evidence of a crime.

Fossil

All traces of past life, even those that have not been petrified.

Gamete

Reproductive cell, also called sex cell, such as sperm and eggs.

Gene

Unit of information of a chromosome; sequence of nucleotides in a DNA molecule that carries out a specific function.

Generation

A "level" in the history of a family or species. There is one generation between parents and children.

Gene Therapy

Treatment of certain diseases of genetic origin by replacing the patient's defective gene(s) with the correct gene(s) to cure the disease.

Genetic Disease

Disease caused partially or wholly by a genetic disorder.

Genetic Engineering

The study of the application of genetics in relation to technological uses.

Geneticist

Scientist who studies genetics.

Genetic Mutation

Error in the copying of a cell's DNA. A few mutations can be beneficial and intensify the cell's original qualities. Mutations are believed to have generated the evolution of species. Most give rise to closed evolutionary lines.

Genetics

The study of DNA and genes.

Genetic Trait

Physical trait transmitted to an organism's descendants, such as hair color and height.

Genome

Complete set of genes of a species.

Haploid

From the Greek term *haplous*, "one"; a cell with only one set of chromosomes, unlike diploid cells. Gametes are haploid cells.

Helix

Geometric spiral shape equivalent to a curve along a cylindrical surface; the shape in which the DNA molecule is curled.

Hemophilia

A group of hereditary diseases caused by the lack of a clotting factor (the most important being Factors VIII and IX). Its most common symptom is spontaneous hemorrhaging.

Heredity

In genetics, all types of genetic material passed on by the parents to a descendant.

Hormone

Glandular secretion with the function of stimulating, inhibiting, or regulating the action of other glands, systems, or organs of the body.

Karyotype

Ordering of the chromosomes of a cell according to shape, number, or size.

Keratin

Protein found in skin, hair, and nails.

Ligase

Protein used by geneticists to join sections of DNA.

Lysosome

Part of the cell that breaks down and reuses worn-out proteins.

Meiosis

Type of double cell division that forms four daughter cells out of one cell, each one with one-half the chromosomes of the original cell; typical in the formation of gametes.

Mitochondria

Cellular organelle that combines food and oxygen to produce energy for the cell.

Mitochondrial DNA

Small amount of DNA contained in the mitochondria of the cell.

Mitosis

Cellular division that produces two genetically identical daughter cells. The most common form of cell division.

Molecule

Minimum quantity into which a substance can be divided without losing its chemical properties. The level immediately below it is the atom.

Monozygotic Twins

Twins who develop from a single zygote that splits in two, forming two genetically identical individuals.

Mummy

Human corpse preserved by artificial methods, which can be preserved for long periods of time. The genetic study of mummies provides much evidence about life in the past.

Natural Selection

Process in which only the organisms that are best adapted thrive and evolve. This selection is carried out without human intervention.

Nitrogenous Base

Type of chemical compound. Four distinct types of bases in DNA make up the genetic code, according to their combinations.

Organelle

Any organ of a cell, including mitochondria, ribosomes, and lysosomes. They carry out specific functions.

Ovule

Female gamete, or sex cell.

Pancreas

Organ that produces insulin, located below the stomach.

PCR (Polymerase Chain Reaction)

Technique for multiplying fragments of DNA using polymerase.

Phenotype

In biology, the visible manifestation of a genotype in a certain environment.

Phylogenetics

The study of evolutionary relationships between the various species, reconstructing the history of their speciation.

Preimplantation Genetic Diagnosis

Method of in vitro selection of embryos based on preferred genetic conditions. They are then implanted in the uterus for normal development.

Protein

Natural or synthetic compound of amino acids, which carries out important functions in an organism.

Radioactivity

Energy given off by certain chemical elements; it can cause genetic alterations or even diseases such as cancer.

Recessive Gene

Gene that, even though present, might or might not be manifested in a pair of alleles depending on the presence of a dominant gene.

Recombinant DNA

Sequence that contains a combination originating from one or more organisms.

Replica

Exact or nearly exact copy of an original. A virus creates replicas of itself after invading a cell.

Repressor

Protein that binds to a DNA chain in order to stop the functioning of a gene.

Reproduction

Sexual or nonsexual creation of other organisms of the same species. The fertilization of gametes is sexual, whereas parthenogenesis is not.

Restriction Enzyme

Protein in certain bacteria that can cut the DNA molecule.

Ribosome

Part of a cell that reads the instructions of the genes and synthesizes the corresponding proteins.

RNA

Ribonucleic acid, similar to DNA but used to transport a copy of DNA code to the ribosome, where proteins are manufactured.

RNA Polymerase

Enzyme that serves as a catalyst for synthe-sizing an RNA molecule based on DNA code.

Selective Breeding

The production of plants or animals that display the results of artificial selection of their genetic traits. Agronomists, veterinarians, and geneticists use selective breeding to improve certain species and breeds or varieties to achieve, for example, greater productivity and crop yields.

Sex Cells

Special cells, also called gametes, with a reproductive function. Some examples are ovules, spermatozoa, and pollen.

Speciation

Evolutionary process in which a new species is formed, for various reasons, from another species.

Species

The lowest unit of classification in evolution. It was originally defined according to the phenotype of each individual. The field of genetics has raised new questions about what constitutes a species.

Spermatozoon (Sperm)

Male gamete or sex cell.

Stem Cell

Cell with the ability to develop into a specific type of cell or bodily tissue. Pluripotent stem cells can develop into any type of cell of the body.

Telomerase

Protein for repairing the telomere of a chromosome. Found only in certain cells.

Telomere

DNA sequence at the end of a chromosome, it is shortened every time the cell divides. The number of times the cell can divide depends on the length of the telomere.

Thymine

One of the four bases that make up DNA, combining in different sequences to form genes.

Transcription

Process of copying a strand of DNA onto a complementary sequence of RNA with the enzyme RNA polymerase.

Transgenic

Describes plants or animals of one species that have undergone genetic modifications using one or more genes from another species.

Vector

In genetic engineering, the agent that introduces a new sequence of DNA into an organism. Viruses and bacteria are often used as vectors.

Virus

Organism composed of DNA or RNA enclosed in a capsid, or protein structure. A virus can invade cells and use them to create more viruses.

X Chromosome

One of the chromosomes that determines a person's sex.

Y Chromosome

Chromosome that determines the male sex; passed on only from fathers to sons.

Zygote

The first cell of a sexually reproduced organism formed from the union of gametes.

For More Information

American Museum of Natural History
Central Park West at 79th Street
New York, NY 10024-5192
(212) 769-5100
Website: http://www.amnh.org
Facebook: @naturalhistory
Twitter: @AMNH
YouTube: American Museum of Natural History
The American Museum of Natural History is a world-renowned scientific and cultural institution. The museum's website includes a variety of information on early human life, evolution, Charles Darwin, and many other topics.

The Charles Darwin Foundation for the Galapagos Islands (CDF)
Puerto Ayora, Santa Cruz Island
Galápagos, Ecuador
(593) 5 2526-146/147
Website: https://www.darwinfoundation.org
Facebook: @darwinfoundation
Twitter: @DarwinFound
YouTube: Charles Darwin Foundation
The CDF is a non-profit organization dedicated to scientific research. The mission of the foundation and its research station is "to provide knowledge and assistance through scientific research and complementary action to ensure the conservation of the environment and biodiversity in the Galapagos Archipelago."

National Museum of Natural History (NMNH)
Smithsonian Institution
Constitution Avenue NW
Washington, DC 20560
(202) 633-1000
Website: https://naturalhistory.si.edu
Facebook: @nmnh.fanpage
Twitter: @NMNH
YouTube: Smithsonian's National Museum of Natural History
The NMNH, part of the Smithsonian Institution, exhibits artifacts and collections on natural history and cultures from around the world. It also provides research materials and offers programs to educate the public. The website includes a great deal of information about evolution and the origins of humankind.

Society for the Study of Evolution
4475 Castleman Avenue
St. Louis, MO 63110-3201
(314) 577-9554
Website: www.evolutionsociety.org
Facebook: @sse.evolution
Twitter: @sse_evolution
The Society for the Study of Evolution aims to promote the study of organic evolution and other related scientific fields. The society holds yearly meetings on evolutionary biology, publishes a scientific journal, and offers educational programs.

For Further Reading

Anderson, Margaret J. Charles Darwin: *Genius of a Revolutionary Theory*. Berkeley Heights, NJ: Enslow Publishers, 2015.

Ardia, Daniel, and Elizabeth Rice. *Evolution*. New York, NY: Cavendish Square, 2014.

Bowler, Peter J. *An Interview with Charles Darwin*. New York, NY: Cavendish Square Publishing, 2015.

Brooker, Robert J. *Conepts of Genetics*. New York, NY: McGraw-Hill Education, 2019.

Brooker, Robert J. *Genetics: Analysis & Principles*. New York, NY: McGraw-Hill Education, 2018.

Gerdes, Louise I. *Human Genetics*. Farmington Hills, MI: Greenhaven Press, 2014.

Huddle, Rusty. *Human Evolution*. New York, NY: Britannica Educational Publishing, 2017.

Johnson, Sylvia A. *Shaking the Foundation: Charles Darwin and the Theory of Evolution*. Minneapolis, MN: Twenty-First Century Books, 2013.

Keranen, Rachel. *Evolution*. New York, NY: Cavendish Square, 2017.

Lewis, Ricki. *Human Genetics: Concepts and Applications*. New York, NY: McGraw Hill Education, 2018.

Lister, Adrian. *Darwin's Fossils: The Collection That Shaped the Theory of Evolution*. Washington, DC: Smithsonian Books, 2018.

Miller, Caitlyn, and Tom Jackson. *Genetics: Why We Are Who We Are*. New York, NY: Cavendish Square, 2018.

Nye, Bill. *Undeniable: Evolution and the Science of Creation*. New York, NY: St. Martin's Press, 2014.

Roberts, Alice. *Evolution: The Human Story*. New York, NY: DK Publishing, 2018.

Webster, Stephen. *Charles Darwin: Naturalist*. New York, NY: Cavendish Square, 2017.

Winston, Robert. *Evolution Revolution*. New York, NY: DK Children, 2016.

Zuchora-Walske, Christine. *Key Discoveries in Life Science*. Minneapolis, MN: Lerner Publications, 2015.

Index